Getting to Market With Your MVP

Getting to Market With Your MVP

How to Achieve Small Business and Entrepreneur Success

J.C. Baker

BEP BUSINESS EXPERT PRESS

Getting to Market With Your MVP: How to Achieve Small Business and Entrepreneur Success

First published in 2018 by
Business Expert Press, LLC
222 East 46th Street, New York, NY 10017
www.businessexpertpress.com

ISBN-13: 978-1-94897-696-1 (paperback)
ISBN-13: 978-1-94897-697-8 (e-book)

Business Expert Press Entrepreneurship and Small Business Management Collection

Collection ISSN: 1946-5653 (print)
Collection ISSN: 1946-5661 (electronic)

Cover and interior design by Exeter Premedia Services Private Ltd., Chennai, India

First edition: 2018

10 9 8 7 6 5 4 3 2 1

Printed in the United States of America.

Abstract

Getting to Market with your MVP "Small Business and Entrepreneur Success" is a book to assist college students, new entrepreneurs, and current business owners in their understanding of how to bring a concept, product, or new business to market. The minimum viable product (MVP) is the foundation of the business and the staple for sustainable growth. Many businesses fail due to the inability of establishing a core concept, or primary product to introduce to the market in a meaningful manner. It is vitally important the business owner is clear about the entry path and the consumer is clear about the product or service being offered. This book is intended to provide a concise method of developing a business strategy for successful entry into the market while eliminating the frustration of trial and error. There are countless variables, obstacles, and barriers inherent in the entrepreneur and small business space. It is a grave oversight to begin a business without having prescribed steps to minimize the risk of ownership. Through this work readers learn the difference between the purpose of a business plan, market analysis, and a feasibility study. Readers will also understand the difference between a good idea and great business model. This book serves as a tool for increasing the opportunity for success when launching a product, service, or a business.

Keywords

business success, entrepreneurs, feasibility, innovativeness, market entry, minimum viable product (MVP), small business, start-up, value proposition

Contents

Introduction

Getting to Market with your MVP "How to Achieve Small Business and Entrepreneur Success" is a book to assist college students, new entrepreneurs, and current business owners in their understanding of how to bring a concept, product, or new business to market. The minimum viable product (MVP) is a foundational aspect of all business and the staple for sustainable growth. Many businesses fail due to the inability of establishing a core concept, or primary product to introduce to the market in a meaningful manner. Many more businesses fail due to the inability to demonstrate meaningful innovation. Innovation is the generation, acceptance, and implementation of new ideas, processes, products, or services used as an instrument to create wealth and gain a competitive advantage in the marketplace (Robbins and O'Gorman 2016). Product innovation is one of the biggest growth drivers for all companies with the ability to add significantly to current markets or create new emerging markets (Murray 2016).

It is vitally important the business owner is clear about the entry path and the consumer is clear about the product or service being offered. This book is intended to provide a concise method of developing a business strategy for successful entry into the market while eliminating the frustration associated with blind trial and error. There are countless variables, obstacles, and barriers inherent in the entrepreneur and small business space. It is a grave oversight to begin a business without having prescribed steps to minimize the risk of ownership. Having a process and knowledge of how to innovate will not guarantee success for any business owner but increase the percentages of success. Readers learn the difference between the purpose of business plans, market analysis, and feasibility studies. Each aspect provides unique details about the market, the product or service, the industry, and the business owner. Readers also understand the difference between a good idea and great business model. A great idea does not denote a great business, while great businesses can be formed out of common or less than stellar ideas. This book serves as a tool for increasing the opportunity for success when launching a product, service, or business.

As the owner of a business consulting firm, I have the opportunity to assist business owners and C-Suite executives with increasing the productivity, efficiency, or overall performance of their respective businesses. In many cases, I am assisting them with bringing new concepts, services, or products to market as a solution for sustainability. Small companies and entrepreneurs have the ability to move quickly in decision-making and course-changing but struggle with finances or the necessary resources to bring the concept to fruition. Larger companies typically have more access to financial resources but take longer to launch or capitalize on the created concepts. In either case, having the best balance, information, and temperament for bringing a new idea, product, or service to market takes high focus, the proper information, diligence, and courage. Many companies struggle with launching new ideas or bringing new products to market. Companies sometimes will scrutinize every decision on how to launch the product from logo designs to product colors. Delayed decision-making in this realm can cause the company to miss the timing of the current trend rendering the new product or concept useless. New entrepreneurs sometimes will launch a product too soon without evidence of need or a legitimate value proposition to the end user.

No matter the stage, launching a product or new concept is a risky proposition. The associated risk should be mitigated as much as possible through sound principles allowing for a greater opportunity for success. High-levels of uncertainty about the future course of the market, delivering customer satisfaction, along with ambiguity about the type and extent of consumer need create an increased risk for successful product launches (Dhebar 2016). Considering the varying degrees of uncertainty, each entrepreneur and small business owner should take the time to assess all facets of product development. Resource shortcomings and scale diseconomies also contribute to the risk for long-term success for small-businesses; therefore appropriate and timely innovation is a key differentiator for viability (Robbins and O'Gorman 2016). The innovation of new product development can be thwarted by epistemic uncertainty which is survival bias and ontic uncertainty which speaks to the changing and disruptive nature of product introduction altering the original nature of the market (Derbyshire and Giovannetti 2017).

To create a holistic approach for understanding how to bring a product or service to market to achieve small business success, a combination of definitions, applicable terms, and an example of real products launched will be used. Each example, term, and concept will provide a vivid picture of the differences in market analysis, feasibility, and the business plan which will ultimately determine if the new idea or product is viable or should be abandoned. The examples demonstrate real-world scenario planning and alternative forecasting leveraging continuing trends for successful entries. Intuitive logic is needed for future product placement considerations along with sound decision-making in the innovative process (Derbyshire and Giovannetti 2017). The level of innovativeness desired by the entrepreneur or small business owner will be highlighted by the detail of execution in the development process. The plan, team, and market trend will play a pivotal role in the overall success of the launch and long-term sustainability.

The experience of launching products begins with the minimum viable product (MVP). As the entrepreneur and small business owner develop the concept of the MVP and execute the created plan accurately, the arrival at the destination of success is not a straightforward path. The entrepreneur will need to examine and re-examine the specifics surrounding the industry, the market, the product, the team, trends, and new emerging knowledge to remain relevant, current, necessary, and valued (Defeng et al. 2017). The behavior of examination and re-examination creates a culture of entrepreneurial orientation comprised of values innovation, manageable risk-taking, and proactiveness to reflect responsible product development in regards to profit earning and MVP success (Chun-Lan 2015). This culture leads to two main activities in new product development and launch which are exploration and exploitation. The exploitation aims to develop profitability through efficiency of business processes, while exploration has the goal of profitability in the medium and long-term through a series of actions in research and development (Jimenez-Jimenez et al. 2018). The relationship between product innovation strategy and new product performance hinges on how the MVP is constructed and launched.

The steps to new product development, launching a new concept, service, or product in the market while ensuring long-term success is not an exact science as every entrepreneur would capitalize in an unimaginable way. This book provides real-life case studies of companies my firm has brought to market or consulted with. These examples demonstrate the main point each chapter illustrates for a holistic understanding of how to develop a new product or service for market entry. The purpose of this book is to provide proven and researched strategies for understanding basic principles surrounding how to get to market with your MVP in a real and tangible way to capture moderate to significant success.

CHAPTER 1

Purpose

Creating a new business or launching a new product in the market is not an easy task or simple objective. The foundation of the launch stems from a concept that someone is connected to emotionally for a host of reasons. Some people become entrepreneurs due to frustration in the traditional work setting, a lack of opportunity to follow passions, the inability to grow, or a perceived need has been identified. The most significant attribute an entrepreneur or small business owner must have is the understanding of their purpose for the new business or product launch. This purpose is the driving force behind the creation of the business or the innovation. The purpose has to be translated into the "why" a business should exist or "why" a product should be launched. The "why" is also connected to "why" does anyone care about the new concept or "why" should they pay attention to "you." The "why" is a complex and multilayered question holding the key to the ultimate success of the business. Entrepreneurs can neglect the idea of relative importance. Just because an idea is essential individually does not denote the importance to a market or a general population. The driving purpose has to be clear from the onset.

Identification of New Ideas

The initial step in creating a new product or a service is the identification of new ideas from different sources. These sources can be experiences and skills possessed by the individual leading them to see their abilities or perceptions as a possible purpose for establishing a new product for market entry. A thorough understanding of a particular field is necessary to identify valuable new ideas effectively with knowledge acquisition requiring greater specialization for its utilization (Defeng et al. 2017). The knowledge, experience, skills, and realization of need push toward the purpose which begins the path for the new products. Some workplace atmospheres promote innovative behaviors through a functional plan accompanied by a set of activities aimed at the generation, development, and implementation of new ideas, products, services, or processes (Jimenez-Jimenez et al. 2018). In today's climate, accelerators and incubators exist to launch an array of new products in the marketplace. Individuals and newly formed companies are selected by larger companies operating as a storehouse for start-ups to "accelerate" their concepts by providing resources and guidance. These accelerators provide the environment for innovativeness and ideation. The innovative behavior is to champion new and valuable concepts as opposed to mimicking the competition in the marketplace.

Entrepreneurs begin their journey from many beginnings. When an employee or a member of an organization becomes frustrated with the operation of their workplace or affiliation, they will often begin thinking of ways to improve products, services, or processes. If there is no method or option to implement those new ideas or demonstrate the ability to integrate them sufficiently, workers will take the risk of embarking on the new concept as a business owner. The mentality takes on a form of self-reliance to fulfill a dream or passion. The risk to bring the new product or service to market is not a deterrent preventing the transition. The purpose can stem from a desire to make a difference in the industry or space the new entrepreneur previously occupied as an employee. The notion to prove a former employer "wrong" or to prove a family member "right" ignites a person to become an entrepreneur. These intrinsic motivational factors can be powerful sources to launch a product or a service; however, these factors will not correctly sustain the product for long-term viability. The purpose behind idea creation or new product development should have more substance, information, programming, and data behind it to create a foundation for growth.

Necessity Drives Purpose

From a small business standpoint, many of the decisions, ideas, and new opportunities derive from the necessity to compete or survive. Small business owners will operate for a short time and recognize they are having difficulty in the marketplace and have to evolve to remain viable.

Changes in the market, laws, regulations, consumer behavior, and many other realities will alter the course of direction for small business owners. In other instances, small business owners will find new ways, methods, or processes of conducting business for the sake of providing quality service for a customer, or by establishing a more efficient method of operation. This discovery spawns the ideation of a new product or concept left wanting development.

An example of this reality is through a franchise company called MasterBlaster® headquartered in Columbus, Ohio. MasterBlaster® is a mobile auto wash company with over 25 years of operation. MasterBlaster® was a small two-person operation set to power blast and wash the exterior of vehicles on automotive dealership lots. Due to new technological advancements, MasterBlaster® was forced to look at their business differently. To maintain the pace of vehicle cleaning without sacrificing quality, the owner of MasterBlaster® created a new and proprietary process for power washing. The revolutionary process allowed for a transition in the overall operation allowing for sustainability in the small business past age, health, and the ability of the owner. MasterBlaster® is now a franchise growing nationwide providing the opportunity for others. The purpose behind this transformation came from the necessity to service the clients at a higher level while combating pressure from competition and a growing market. The English-language proverb states, "necessity is the mother of all invention," which argues need is a primary purpose of inventing. Necessity may spawn new ideas, but it does not guarantee business success. However, having a deeply rooted need benefiting multiple stakeholders is the onset of a successful product or service.

Struggle for Innovation and Purpose

As simple as these discoveries may appear through the natural course of work and providing services, many entrepreneurs, and small business owners struggle with innovation and purpose. A businessperson seeks the unmet need or will create an entirely new need as they design a method of how to satisfy the need for the benefit of the stakeholders while also monetizing the need (Štefan and Branislav 2016). New entrepreneurs and small business owners alike will create a new concept in the early stages without reflecting on the real purpose or the strategy for the concept lead-ing them to dysfunction, direction, or misalignment. One of the most important principles for any business is to create profit for sustainability. Determining a need for business may not denote the ability to monetize. One portion of providing value to the stakeholders are identifying the stakeholders and game-planning how each party will realize the benefit. This level of meta-cognition or thought may be missing from the entre-preneur or small business owner.

An illustration of this reality is a young entrepreneur from the Midwest looking to create a digital platform to enhance the relational interaction of larger companies with their end users. The need was adequately artic-ulated as it is reasonable to believe consumers would like to experience excellent customer service when interacting in retail to encourage addi-tional spending. Necessity, experience, and skill in digital development guided the purpose. The failure came with the purpose of who was to benefit financially and how to monetize the platform. Without having the economic structure purposed for viability, the platform did not make a significant impact in the marketplace to create the value it was initially intended to accomplish.

Viewing from the perspective of establishing a business or enhancing an existing one is the purpose of any new concept. The purpose of a new product, service, or process should have more components than merely sensationalized connection, bias, or personal gratitude. The emotions con-nected with these components can lead to misdiagnosed product place-ment, overestimation, and false beliefs of success. Business professionals need to solve problems, make sound decisions, and apply creativity using specialized theoretical and factual knowledge to benefit all stakeholders associated with the new concept, product, or service (Ashley et al. 2016). When the purpose of the new product development is a sensationalized concept or a self-serving product, the chances for failure increase due to market misrepresentation. As entrepreneurs look to establish a new busi-ness, the purpose will determine the foundation of creation. Many busi-nesses have been launched and closed on the premise of a selfish motive of pride, ego, or just because of the inability to work for an appointed leader. Poor calculations and decision-making predicated on dreams, illusions, and wishful thinking can permeate. Established businesses cannot afford for appointed leaders to operate in a sensationalized method of purpose for the sake of the stakeholders. An example of sensationalized purpose came from a client motivated by highlighting the need to eliminate food deserts in urban areas by creating ethnically led investments for ethnically based brick and mortar. The passion for elevating black-owned business while reducing food deserts in urban cities was the driving purpose. The most significant issue with this purpose as the guiding force was the lack of understanding surrounding the food industry, the grocery space, urban purchasing behaviors, along with the economic benefit to all stakeholders. The only parameter accounted for was personal passion and the dream of creating paradigms. The new ideas must be purposed to elevate the operation of the business in a uniformed fashion allowing for the stakeholders to benefit in all realms articulated as progress.

Categories for New Product Development

Consumer-facing or company-facing are also categories for new product development. Consumer-facing products, services, and processes are designed with the intent to alter, enhance, or redirect how the consumer engages with the company. Consumer-facing developments tend to derive from reviews, beta-testing, and market analysis. The entrepreneur or small-business owner will receive feedback from the consumer/customer base leading to new conclusions to refine, enrich, or improve the products or services offered. In consumer perspective, new product development is considered as something that is perceived as having the ability to give a significant and meaningful impact for producing real consumption in a particular market (Husen 2017). The consumer must recognize the new product or service as having functional, experiential, symbolic, or brand value to increase the purchase or interaction intent (Husen 2017). Entrepreneurs and small business owners will create and develop products/services in ways suggesting increased interaction when the strategy is consumer-facing. When a retailer removes the barriers of lines for check-out procedures and reducing wait-time, the purpose of this innovation is considered to be consumer-facing although there are benefits for the company as a whole. The benefit to the company is a faster turnover in customer traffic, better-perceived purchasing experience leading to increased return shopping, and employees can spend efforts enhancing other aspects of the business such as inventory, customer service, and cleaning to name a few.

Exploration and Exploitative Elements

Another way to view the purpose of new product development is through the elements of exploration and exploitative methods. Exploration includes aspects such as searching, variation, risk-taking, experimentation, flexibility, discovery, and innovation as exploitation speaks to refinement, choices, production, efficiency, selection, implementation, and execution (Chun-Lan 2015). The entrepreneur and small business owner will provide a good foundation for new product development if they understand if they are utilizing exploration or exploitative methods for their concept or services. As business owners journey through the exploration of new product development, they will need to transition from self-serving perspectives to system perspectives of analyzing resources and capacities to solve problems or provide value (Muff 2017). If the purpose is to work through the creative process to find a need or new method of operation, the purpose will have to be coupled with a purpose to add sustainability. From an exploitative method entrepreneur or small business owner will concentrate on the technical purposes of new product development for market entry. The positive impact of business is not solely measured economically, or ideologically but holistically assessing the relevant contributions for noticeable improvement or change (Muff 2017). The purpose of new product development from the exploration or exploitative mindset is similar when vetting the concept or looking to test the theory of the concept. An example of this dichotomy is a 501c3 nonprofit organization looking to generate revenue more than providing the service for the target audience. This particular organization reported that stakeholder profits guided the decision to sell the company to a buying interest in contrast to not prioritizing charitable giving in a manner consistent with the original mission and vision (Badgett 2018). Through exploration, the purpose of a new product or service to market may appear as one aspect just as that same product or service may look completely different and unrecognizable through the exploitative process. It is also not uncommon for a new product or service to undergo both the exploration and the exploitative process for a more broad view of entry. In either example, the business strategy and the business model will become the conduits for success.

Business Model and Business Strategy Purpose

The purpose of a new product or service will become more glaringly apparent after a robust business strategy and business model has been created. A business model and strategy are two essential preconditions and fundamentals of a company's existence leading to the implementation of the concept and transforming the concept into reality (Štefan and Branislav 2016). The initial purpose of the new product development can create barriers or gaps in the business model and the business strategy. An ambitious and passionate business strategy cannot be coupled with a poor business model, and neither shall the reciprocal take place. The relationship between the two must be aligned to reinforce the overall theme of the purpose and allow for the new product to come forth. One primary key inside of the business strategy and business model is the view on returns back to the company. The entrepreneur and small business owner may view success as a return on investment, return on innovation, return on implementation, or a return on interaction (Whole Brain Thinking 2017). This Whole Brain Thinking approach to the purpose of new product development can be interacted as a single approach for each aspect of return or work together combining multiple returns to pursue a new product. The acknowledgment of the return is one direct purpose leading toward decision-making, trends, marketing efforts, strategy, recognition of confounds, level of engagement, and overall entry expectations (Gill et al. 2017). Frequently new entrepreneurs may be persuaded to create a new product, service, or business with the purpose of only concentrating on the return on investment or the return on innovation. This specialized focus can create issues in implementation or interaction returns which can ultimately cause for failure in the new venture or business. Conversely, a heavy focus on interaction and implementation can also forsake monetization or uniqueness which can also lead to failure. Analyzing each component of return and comparing to the purpose associated with each return will assist in a more well-thought-out product. A broad and vague purpose can be borderless and challenging to defend among the market, stakeholders, and even the team needed to bring the new product to market (Houlder and Nandkishore 2016). The entrepreneur has to be conscious as to how their purpose of product creation will fit holistically for a better survival rate in the marketplace.

Case Study: Two Apparel Companies

Company A: Slogan Shirt Company

Slogan Shirt Company (company name withheld for the illustration) was a concept brand apparel company looking to launch a brand of t-shirts, hoodies, and hats with a slogan as the lead the value proposition for consumers. We will call the slogan "I Am a Gift" for the illustration. The entrepreneur and the business partner believed the slogan had personal meaning in their life and it would be a great idea to create a clothing line with the slogan representing the mentality behind the apparel. The articulated idea is others would recognize their stronger inner self, and the message would inspire others to be the best version of themselves when faced with obstacles, trials, and opposition. The messaging was to provide an uplifting attitude when consumers would wear the gear as they exercise, go out for a night on the town, or go to work in a casual setting. When posed questions of how would they monetize the product in a meaningful way or how would they connect with their audience, the responses were incomplete and not consistent. The intrinsic connection to the slogan and the personal meaning the slogan carried through their individual lives demonstrated a sensationalized purpose. This rationale is not a poor indication of "why" the brand should be created, but there was no additional purposing surrounding the apparel brand. As the recommendations for market-entry began to appear, it became apparent they did not have a sustainable business strategy or a viable business model. The purpose for new product development and entry was for personal reasons from a company-facing view although it originally appeared to be customer-facing as the product was meant to "uplift" others.

Company B: Gradu8 Inc.®

Gradu8 Inc.® is a three-pronged company operating as an apparel company, promotional product company, and a 501c3 nonprofit organization specializing in providing resources for students at all levels while bringing awareness and an attitude of completion to all. This messaging of completion is conducted through the Evolution of Knowledge which markets to graduates from pre-school through the doctorate level. The apparel boasts slogans and designs with academic, graduation, and achievement innuendos. The promotional products are a conduit for supplying schools, institutions, and businesses with products needed to function. The 501c3 nonprofit organization Motivate to Gradu8® provides resources such as finances, motivational speakers, success summits, and bereavement counseling to students in need. As a foundational principle, every purchase will earmark eight percent of profits to the school of the patron's choice. The original intent and purpose of the business owner were to highlight and popularize the notion of graduating as he was the first member in his family to attend a four-year institution and ultimately graduate.

Figure 1.1 *Gradu8 Apparel® represented in the marketplace*

The purpose was personal, intrinsic, and sensationalized by the owner. The difference between Gradu8 Inc.® and the Slogan Shirt Company is developing a consumer-facing process, strategy, and model around the purpose driven company.

Chapter 1 Review

1. Understand the "why"
2. Define the purpose
3. Distinguish between consumer-facing or company-facing purpose
4. Exploration or exploitative aspects drive purpose
5. The business strategy and business model highlight purpose
6. Returns on investment, innovation, implementation, and interaction connect purpose

CHAPTER 2

Recognizing Opportunity

Every entrepreneur and small business owner must operate with a purpose to achieve success for their company or concept. The next step in the progression is recognizing if there is an opportunity to leverage the new product or service. Identifying the opportunity and exercising the correct timing will make the difference between a successful entry and an immediate failure. Some ideas are fantastic for an industry or market, but if the opportunity to enter the market has closed, the idea is no longer relevant. There are many ways an entrepreneur can recognize an opportunity in the marketplace. Meta-cognition, personal consumerism, problem-solving behavior, active listening, and industry trends are all methods for the entrepreneur to determine how to enter into the market with new product development. Entrepreneurs and small business owners will benefit by viewing the world from various perspectives stemming from personal experience and expertise. Meta-cognition is the reflection about the thoughts and actions leading toward choices, engaging, interaction, and behavior (Ahmad 2017). The collective thoughts and experiences of the small business owner provide background information on the needs and trends of the consumer surrounding the space the entrepreneur occupies. When individuals focus on the issues in familiar industries and have solutions, opportunities for product entry arise. The key for any entrepreneur is to be aware of market indicators, changes, and disruptions to take advantage of emerging opportunities or avoid potentially harmful activity.

Understanding Business Opportunity

An entrepreneurial business opportunity is a perceived means of generating economic value not previously exploited and not currently realized by others emphasizing the newness and innovative characteristics (Santos et al. 2018). The notion of every new concept not currently represented in a specific market is an opportunity misconception held by new entrepreneurs. This misnomer does not include the economic component leading to additional frustration and ruin. To identify a business opportunity the entrepreneur has to perceive connections between apparently unrelated events, trends, and behaviors and changes in aspects such as technology, demographics, market, government, or policies in a meaningful pattern to determine as a legitimate opportunity (Santos et al. 2018). The purpose of the new concept, product, or service has to match the changes in the industry. The relationship of previous knowledge, information, and life experiences reducing uncertainty connected with the discovery of innovation is how entrepreneurial opportunities are generally recognized (Atsan 2016). The entrepreneur is leaning on the previous knowledge and experiences to determine sustainability. Sustainable entrepreneurship is a way to generate a competitive advantage by recognizing new products, methods, markets, and processes while conventional entrepreneurship (Ploum et al. 2018). Having a good sense of the value proposition, a normative concept, and a method to unveil the development in a way to make an appropriate economic, social, and environmental connection is vital. Previous personal failures and successes are a portion of the experiences leading to opportunity recognition. Market failures alone should be confused with opportunities themselves as opportunities are connected with the action of performing in a manner leading to productivity (Ploum et al. 2018). The reflection of failure generates from an objective or subjective perspective, and the recognition of opportunity will have to combine both perceptions from first-hand data and experience. People are more likely to exploit opportunities if developed information from previous employment is used allowing for better coping with liabilities, reduction of obstacles, and uncertainties related to launching a new product (Atsan 2016). A critical analysis of previous experiences in the workplace or industry is an excellent tool for understanding the opportunity in a market.

Opportunity Evaluation

The reflection and analysis of these experiences and meta-cognition surrounding new product development is an in-depth cognitive perspective deriving from a conscious mental process. Entrepreneurial cognition is the knowledge structures people use to make assessments, judgments, or decisions involving opportunity evaluation and venture creation (Santos et al. 2018). The assessments and judgments of products or services have to be critical and holistic. An example of this critical analysis comes through The Movement Sports and Enrichment Organization. The Movement® founding principles are providing programming around city youth through sports, mentoring, and confidence building. The Movement® was not original in their thought to assist youth in need of role models and a safe place to interact, but the operation, delivery, and branding had to be original to create high-level interest. The Movement® was initially constituted as a for-profit entity and later transitioned into a 501c3 nonprofit organization. The founder of The Movement® was a school teacher, a fitness trainer, and a little league coach. His personal experiences combined with problem-solving behavior and market trends led to the purpose of creating a service to program around disadvantaged youth in urban areas. The formal meta-cognition process revealed an opportunity to create an inclusive youth program, diverse and wide-ranging with a separate component specializing in the emotional needs of young girls, and a "University" curriculum model. The business opportunity surrounding the transition of the business model of The Movement® is the number of potential corporate partnerships due to the female programming component and the "University" model offering. Many companies in the region sought new and worthwhile organizations to sponsor while providing opportunities for members of their serving communities. This change in paradigm allowed for additional satellite locations, increased staffing, additional youth programming, more revenue, and more strategic partners. The opportunity as a for-profit athletic-based company was not as sustainable as the 501c3 non-profit model.

Sustainability for Opportunity

Sustainability is one of the goals of new product development when entering the market. Seizing the opportunity for a successful product or service market entry will hinge on aspects related to stability, consistency, and predictability rather than the uncertainty and constant change associated with the entrepreneurial activity (Santos et al. 2018). An opportunity can only be viewed as an opportunity if it can display stability and consistency among the end users while providing value for all stakeholders. The start of the entrepreneurial process begins with the identification of potential business ideas that can be explored for future development and monetized (Ploum et al. 2018). The entrepreneur and small business owner will need to employ "out-of-the-box" thinking to create a new image for operation, development, or market entry. The opportunity recognition stage is not the result of a random thought or dream, but a conscious meta-cognition will deliberate thought surrounding the industry or market of choice. Collaborative filtering approaches, portfolio analyses, and association mining techniques are practices used in the early stages of opportunity recognition (Lee and Lee 2017). An opportunity has to represent multiple aspects of the business, and therefore the consideration of economic, technical, and interaction value propositions are paramount. Opportunity recognition depends on an active and engaged analysis of an environment, experimentation of solutions to problems, learning by doing, and critically reflecting on theories connected to real-life situations (Santos et al. 2018). There is typically no single idea leading toward the development of a new product or service, but a string of ideas from experiences, issues, and market trends combining to form a new perspective. Economic, technical, and interactive considerations determine if an idea translates into an opportunity. A customized innovation process works best to account for misalignment in market analysis, prevention of product bias, and increased quality execution (Robbins and O' Gorman 2016).

Customized Innovation Process

A customized innovation process also assists with the ability to forecast future demands which is crucial for recognizing an opportunity. Two ways to forecast the demands for a future opportunity are using existing markets with known measures of demand such as the number of customers, units consumed, and revenue dollars along with estimated annual growth and behavior rates (Dhebar 2016). The calculation of future market behavior is a fundamental step for small business owners. A good idea today may not be as strong of an idea one year from now. The competency, skill, and task ability of the entrepreneur or small business owner will be tested by not just the current capabilities but the future considerations as well. If a concept or service is unable to scale, adjust, or adapt to the future needs of the market, then the opportunity is rendered void. For instance, there appears to be an opportunity in the business world to enhance the experience of the U.S. Postal service by improving the transactional process of letters and bill payments. An entrepreneur may believe creating a kiosk to process letters, complete bill payments, and send acknowledgments will fulfill the need in the market based on experience, observation, and customer response. However, e-mail and online bill pay have covered much of the technological need for patrons looking to improve speed and convenience. The behavior of in-person postal transactions derives from the need for packaging and large product. Large carriers such as the U.S. Postal Service, UPS, DHL, and FedEx govern the behavior of in-person transactions. The opportunity would exist with enhancing their abilities as opposed to recreating the same vehicles of e-mail or autopay.

Innovation projects exist in three distinct stages consisting of discovery, incubation, and acceleration (Robbins and O'Gorman 2016). These three phases also help identify new opportunities to foster new product development. The discovery comes from the realization of market trends and solutions to problems for a particular industry. During the discovery phase, many questions about the innovation, implementation, and interaction emerge. The discovery questions are in the form of "what market, for who, and why do they care?" Answers to these fundamental questions set the occasion for recognizing an opportunity in the marketplace. The incubation and acceleration stages are the actions behind the verification of an opportunity in the market. The knowledge accumulated before the incubation and acceleration stages are crucial to success in recognition of opportunity. The breadth of knowledge an entrepreneur has on a diversified customer base along with multiple market segments will determine the barriers to innovation or the success for entry (Defeng et al. 2017). Every barrier and obstacle existing in the new product development and launch sequence are unknown at the onset. Outlining as many barriers to entry during the idea stage is an essential step for increasing the percentages of success during the opportunity recognition phase. Considering innovation involves creativity, initiation, and the discovery of novel concepts it is impossible to determine all levels of obstacles when looking to capitalize on a new opportunity in the market (Robbins and O'Gorman 2016). The meta-cognition displayed in this level contributes to experiential learning consisting of creating knowledge by transforming experience to four learning processes including feeling, reflective observation, abstract conceptualization, and active experimentation (Santos et al. 2018). Experiential learning adds to the knowledge of the entrepreneur assisting with the ability to recognize an opportunity in business by considering different potentialities and ideas in the first stage. This learning and realization of knowledge is a crucial element for proper product development and market entry.

Demand Uncertainty

Recognizing opportunity in the marketplace is made difficult through confounds of demand uncertainty. The perceived opportunity by the small business owner will have to appropriately connect with the demand displayed by the potential end user. Questions to consider while determining a new opportunity are as follows:

1. Are end-user needs met?
2. Iʋw will the product be altered in the future?
3. Will the market understand the introduced development?
4. How quickly can the innovation spread in the form of awareness?
5. How large is the market?

Significant uncertainties concerning a new product to market are as follows:

- End user issues that the new product may solve.
- The perceived need may convert to wants changing the demand for the product or service.
- As trade-offs become apparent, the end user's interaction can morph into unrecognized behavior.
- The evolution of other emerging technology and concepts can change the interactive behavior of the end user.

All of these levels of uncertainty surround the socio-economic factors and forces in the market (Derbyshire and Giovannetti 2017). To be prepared for uncertainty in the market, political, economic, social, technological, environmental, and legal considerations must exist. The changes in these forces can be unpredictable and diverse which is also amplified by the introduction of innovation (Jimenez-Jimenez et al. 2018). Developing contingency options predicted on multiple conditions and variables inherent in the market will bode well for the entrepreneur when exploring new opportunities. These contingencies relate to execution plans, environmental changes, and end-user response (Chun-Lan 2015). As the promises of an opportunity alter with increasing realities of uncertainty and change, the contingency derived from knowledge and high-level meta-cognition will prove useful.

Case Study: Two Beverage Companies

Company A: A Water Company

A water company (actual name withheld) was a company looking to specialize in filtered water systems to increase the health content of everyday drinking water for families and businesses. The mentality behind the systems was to assist with the paradigm shift of purifying drinking water in a particular method to reduce illness, ailments, and reduce the overall cost of purchasing bottled water. The perceived opportunity was attached to a mentality of health and wellness within the shopping, food & beverage, and fitness industries. The goal was to capitalize on the health movement to fight obesity and reduce medical costs associated with poor health conditions. The uncertainties existed around the proprietary delivery system of the water, the marketing for brand awareness, and the education to the end-user to realize the benefits. The value proposition directly correlates to the health benefits for the end user as there is no commercial value for the product. The product was a multiple thousand dollar commitment to the end user but would ultimately save the end user tens of thousands of dollars over the time of ownership. The confounds from high pricing, market confusion, and low visibility reduced the possibility of exploiting an opportunity in the market.

Company B: Role Tea

Role Tea is an iced tea blend featuring turmeric and ginger as the health qualities in the beverage. The purpose of Role Tea is to combat sugary drinks by providing a healthier alternative without sacrificing taste. The opportunity realized is capitalizing on the paradigm shift of health and wellness in the United States. Other products have entered the market to offer supplements to the traditional tea market, but none have boasted the health benefits of Role Tea. Alternative drink companies such as Bai and Honest Tea have found significant success in the food and beverage market; however, they still allowed an opportunity for an even healthier product. Role Tea was able to take advantage of the opportunity in the tea market by adding the elements of turmeric and ginger combined with flavors such as apple, mango, peach, and lemon. Unlike the Company A, "The Water Company," the delivery method and interaction with the end user was recognizable and familiar. Role Tea can now be purchased online and in retail stores such as Whole Foods and Wegmans. The product was sampled in multiple regions nationwide and originally placed in small "mom and pop" shops for validation. The larger retailers were able to see the merit and value of the product which led to increased opportunities and sales. The end users were able to buy Role Tea in the same manner as their other favorite or other popular drinks. Instead of an educational

Figure 2.1 Role Tea® represented with Whole Foods Market®
drinkroletea.com

Figure 2.2 Role Tea® represented commercially and in the market

overhaul and significant financial contribution by the consumer, Role Tea was able to capitalize on the same opportunity of health and wellness in a manner more acceptable to the general public.

Chapter 2 Review: Recognition for Opportunity

1. Meta-cognition, personal experiences, problem-solving behavior, and industry trends are ways to recognize opportunity
2. Evaluate measures for sustainability and value when assessing opportunity
3. A customized innovation process will allow for appropriate opportunity recognition
4. Demand uncertainty increase barriers in new product development always exist with new opportunities

CHAPTER 3

Concept Creation— Defining the Dream

As a business consultant, encounters with many people with ideas for a business or how to grow their existing company abound. Defining the concept or the dream is a difficult step for the majority of them. The previous chapters discussed the purpose of a new concept and how to recognize if there is an opportunity for the new concept. This chapter assists in understanding how to appropriately determine if the purpose and the opportunity lead to a sustainable concept for market entry. A classic misconception is a useful purpose and opportunity means the concept fits the need appropriately. With a definite purpose and market opportunity, the entrepreneur or small business owner has to create the proper concept to provide a suitable solution. The ability to innovate effectively is the single most crucial factor in developing and sustaining competitive advantage with new product development as it is essential for survival and success (Robbins and O'Gorman 2016).

Define the Dream

The dream or the concept of an entrepreneur may be fit to create a new business, add a product, or merely serve as a hobby. The goal of developing a new product is to ensure the effort matches the expectation for what it is created to achieve. The business owner has to determine the definition of the concept created. Each product, concept, or service creates either a functional or symbolic value. Functional value refers to performance improvement directly resulting from adopting while the symbolic value is derived through signaling effects (Grover et al. 2018). In either case, the impact on individuals, organizations, and the society are measured through the functional aspects of market share and financial performance while the symbolic aspects are realized in a positive brand image, reputation, and mitigating environmental pressure (Grover et al. 2018). The business owner needs to know if the concept creation provides the direction of value or a combination of value. Entrepreneurs may view the concept as an image builder, strategic transformer, reactive defender, or a performance enhancer (Grover et al. 2018). As a published author, the previously written three books were a product of image building, strategic transforming, and performance enhancing. The example is timely as many new authors have a story to tell hence the reason they would like to put the story into print, but they rarely have a process or a prescribed value proposition in mind. The first book Common Sense "How Much Does It Cost?" was written to build the personal brand and add credibility to the unique thought process illustrated in the professional work. The second book, God Made You Perfect, "A Believer's Guide to Perfection" was written as a strategic transformer for faith-based organizations. The third book Business Leader Success, "An Introduction to Elite Business Leaders" Vol. 3 is a performance enhancer for the intended target audience. The example highlights how all three works were books to share with the world, but the purpose, opportunity, and direction of the concept were completely different.

While a business owner is looking to define their concept, indicators exist to provide guidance. An indicator can be used to synthesize information for decision-making regarding the action or improvement needed for concept creation (Mata-Lima et al. 2016). These indicators will provide signs of changes in the environmental, social, and economic climate for the benefit of the business owner. An example of an indicator is how Amazon® has changed the distribution channel of products to make them more convenient and quicker to access. There was a time where big-box retailers such a Toys R Us® and K-Mart® were the primary methods of obtaining a product. Amazon® designed innovation to alter how consumer purchased and interacted with their products. Watching the incline of Amazon® is an indicator of how a new product should be created to compete in current and future market.

The indicators manifest in multiple dimensions for the business owner to be aware of concerning concept creation. The first dimension is the content of the concept which refers to the strategic change, the process dimension concerns with how to conduct change, and the context dimension refers to the conditions through the concept is made (Grover et al. 2018). These dimensions lead to a higher-level of focus for concept creation. The meta-cognition employed in this stage will connect to the indicators providing a broader scope for goal-seeking. The target of the indicators and the dimensions are the organizational performance, business process, customer experience, and market enhancement (Grover et al. 2018). The concept created must have a goal of enhancing the performance of the organization due to the need for innovation to provide sustainability opportunities. The business process must be conducive to the concept created to ensure proper introduction to the market. Lastly, the result is the customer experiencing the innovation in a manner that feels innovative to them. All of these targets are interrelated and extend from the identification of the indicators pointing to needed innovation.

The product, process, and organizational innovation are three types of innovation to be cognizant of during the discovery and concept creation process. Product innovation is the commercialization of a significantly improved or entirely new product, process innovation is the introduction of a new or significantly improved method, and organizational innovation is new or significantly improved management or business practice (Souto 2015). Each one of these three innovation types is accompanied by indicators and dimensions to assist in the concept creation process. The considerations for the type of innovation are similar and in some cases may intertwine as one complete strategy of innovation. As an example of this reality, a client of the firm has a product called the TG-30® which significantly changes how conveyor belts in manufacturing companies operate. The TG-30® reduces the point of contact with conveyor belts during emergency stops and maintenance dramatically reducing the potential of accidents and safety issues in a manufacturing plant. This product also doubles as a process as the method of training and execution has been altered to maximize the safety opportunities the TG-30® provides. This product also has ramifications on the organization has supervisors, and managers can assume new roles within the manufacturing company due to the capabilities of risk-reducing opportunities the TG-30® will offer. In cases where multiple employees were responsible for the supervision of the safety features, this TG-30® will eliminate the need for job duplication allowing for the human capital to maximize another facet of the business.

As innovation separates into three kinds, the degree of novelty categorizes innovation. Radical and incremental innovation are the two ways innovation can be viewed to assist business owners with concept creation. Radical innovation is a process of creative destruction, revolutionary change, and a breakthrough in products, processes, or service while incremental innovation has less risk and provides improvements of previous products, processes, or services (Souto 2015). It is possible for innovation to begin as incremental and through trial and error becomes radical with the exposure to new information or stimulus. To illustrate this reality the notable hair loss product Rogaine® was discovered by chance as testing was for other indications of minoxidil and the side effects for the studies was the signs of regrowing hair (Choi et al. 2018). The entrepreneur will be better inclined to recognize opportunities and direction when they understand the type of innovation they embark on combined with a comprehension of the indicators, dimensions, and targets for the concept creation.

Stakeholder Collaboration

How the business owner defines the concept, strategically creates the concept, and articulates the concept is vital for stakeholder comprehension. A well-thought-out concept combined with a poorly communicated strategy will lead to failure in the market. The definition and process of new product development have resonated with the target audience and the stakeholders affected by the innovation. The core concept relies on stakeholder collaboration which includes entities such as research organizations, government, clients, consumers, suppliers, and organizational members while linking the financial, material resources, information, and knowledge for a shared-value innovation (Banu et al. 2016). Although the entrepreneur or small business owner may believe the origin of the concept through the identification of purpose and recognition of opportunity exists solely within themselves, the development of the concept becomes a general consideration among many groups. The new concept must apply to all levels of interaction through the pillars of collaboration, idea sharing, value adding to enhance the competitive advantage and to detract risks related to innovation activity (Banu et al. 2016). Therefore, as the entrepreneur is working to define the concept, the consideration must include all layers of the stakeholders for a holistic approach.

Every layer of collaboration could mean the difference between a successful entry and a failed launch. A stakeholder is someone affected by the existence of the company. Entrepreneurs can perform as self-facing or company-facing entities. It is simple to be consumed by the idealistic nature of a new concept, service, or product when in the idea creation stage. However, the stakeholders have to embrace the same enthusiasm by sharing in the value of the new product in a meaningful way. Investors would like to a return on their investment therefore the monetization model is crucial for their participation in the new product development. Collaboration between the investor and the business owner is necessary to provide the proper financial resources for market entry.

Laws, regulations, appropriate licenses, and certifications are critical for creating a concept as failures in these areas could lead to infringements, fines, and lawsuits. The governmental and legal stakeholder partners assist in ensuring the protection of the product, compliance, and legal adherence for less risky product development. When concepts emerge having an understanding of patents, trademarking, copyrights and registration allow for the business owner to determine the level of protection for their product or to protect from violating another businesses claims. These aspects can be as broad as infringing on design, utility, logo, brand marking, or a name. If the competitive advantage for the created concept is already in used, claimed, or identified, the business owner has to make alterations or changes. The burden of proof is on the business owner to ensure the new concept is, in fact, new or at least differentiated enough to prevent legal battles or "cease and desist" orders.

Material resource stakeholders are critical to the physical development of the concept. Collaboration and partnership with individuals, companies, and suppliers with the ability to source build, provide raw materials, and add to the supply chain are invaluable to the overall scope of concept creation. If a business owner has an innovative idea but cannot physically recreate the concept, then the attempt for market entry will fall flat. The materials for a concept cannot be complicated to access or duplicate for the opportunity of a successful concept creation for market entry. In some cases, the resources needed are available but only accessible in large quantities which may not bode well for the concept. The producer of the material or the provider of the logistical service would have to benefit in a manner commensurate with their individual business needs for the business owner to realize a successful launch. An example of this reality is through our apparel company Gradu8 Inc.® The fabric, embroidery, screen-printing, labeling, packaging, along with the supply chain have to benefit each company to deliver one shirt to a patron. For the development of one item, there are many layers of operations needed to perform and compensate correctly. Each one of these compartmental layers needs to be accounted for as a benefit to the stakeholders to deem the new concept as a good concept. In this same example, if it costs $40 to benefit each material stakeholder and the business owner can only price the product at $20 to accommodate the demand of the market, it is clear the concept does not make sense in the marketplace.

The client and consumer stakeholders have to understand and appreciate the new product. A business owner can drive the company with a purpose, recognize the opportunity with great timing, have a plan to develop the product, but will fail if the consumer market does not adequately understand the product. The client and consumer stakeholder is the primary purpose for innovative thought and should lead the charge in new product development. The concept created has to be consumer-facing in such a manner the target audience will not only understand the innovation but also operate as a conduit for increasing awareness and "buy-in." A business owner will lose if their concept does not resonate with the target audience in design or utility. Tesla® was able to demonstrate this reality very well since the emergence of their vehicle technology. Tesla has been able to encapsulate the electric plug-in market at a higher rate than traditional electric plug-in vehicle makers such as Toyota, Nissan, and Chevrolet due to design and utility geared more toward the everyday shopper and technological advances (Vogan 2017). Although Tesla has existed as a company for less time than the traditional powers, their ability to reflect the desire and expectation of the current market has allowed them to catapult passed their competition. The client and

consumer stakeholders have responded to the representation of the Tesla®
brand among their hedonic appeal.

Overall, the discovery phase of the new product development or concept creation has to include the consideration of all stakeholders. The
business owners meta-cognition should explore the needs and wants of
each stakeholder to be mindful of ways to interact with them in a significant and meaningful way. The concept will not merely satisfy the creative
desire of the entrepreneur but provide value to anyone associated with the
new concept. The goal is to create a universal and diverse product with
benefits to a wide range of stakeholders.

New Concept and Business Model

The first realization for an entrepreneur or small business owner is to
understand the new concept has to have a business model accompany the
development. The concept is the focal point but does not translate to the
market without a model to catapult it. Business models describe ratio-
nales how owners create, deliver, capture value, and process the new concept and execute the strategy (Prause 2015). The business model creates
new options for applying and exploiting knowledge and technology in
different methods than the competition, while also providing a platform
for understanding and visibility (Souto 2015). Deliberation during the
development stage leads to the identification of strategic supply, demand
drivers, macroeconomic environment, trends, technological readiness,
financial considerations, infrastructure, distribution channels, essential
resources, strategic partnerships, and customer segments (Prause 2015).
The concept does not provide value alone but only through the integration of each component mentioned. The concept is to provide innovation for the company but can only accomplish the goal if accounting for
significant aspects of market entry. Just as the business owner is critically
thinking about the design of the new concept individually, equal consideration is due to all of the drivers of product development.

The business owner's knowledge base will be the leading factor of
progress in the concept creation stage. Education, experience, programming, and guidance generate the knowledge base for the business
owner. All of these methods are useful when looking to develop a new

product for market entry. Knowledge innovation and knowledge management coincide to create new ventures with the assistance of a reliable business model. Human capital, technological assets, market assets, and infrastructure assets make up the knowledge assets of an entrepreneur (Wei 2017). The business model allows the business owner to build around the thoughts concerning the stakeholders in a tangible way. The concept will need a reliable business model to account for all of the aspects encountered during market entry. A product line must be designed and scheduled so significant considerations such as market requirements, future constraints, time to market and product features are taken into account (Goswami and Tiwari 2015). As an example of this reality, Role Tea® underwent a flavor change based on consumer stakeholder recommendation. Mango replaced the original flavor of Cinnamon as a more mellow and softer taste according to organized consumer feedback. Sourcing, proper beverage alignment, and ingredient constitution to maintain the same standard of freshness, taste, and health benefits make changing the mango flavor a complex task. If access to the mango fruit diminishes, then Role Tea® suffers in the delivery demands and shelving requirements. This reality affects every entity in the supply chain along with the retailers expecting to sell the product. The perceived functional importance of the product feature is driven by the customer evaluation which can include attainable speed and product quality (Goswami and Tiwari 2015). The model surrounding the business must be sound for successful concept creation. Obstacles and barriers down the road have to be planned from the beginning to increase the percentages of success. The product life-cycle, design, development, operations, logistics, supply chain management, and cross-company interconnectivity make up essential aspects in the business model which are also synonymous with concept creation (Prause 2015). The business owner will need to analyze relevant knowledge and information of not only the product or concept but also all of the business factors responsible for market entry.

Business Strategy Versus Business Model

The business model allows for a business owner to put a system or a method in place for the new concept creation and market entry. If the business model is nonexistent or incoherent, then the concept can suffer due to ambiguity in market entry. A business strategy is a plan to improve the position in the market or industry by guiding to confront or avoid competitors (Štefan and Branislav 2016). The strategy is the plan of attack based on verifiable information, collected data, and trend analysis to match the creation of the concept. A strategy for a product could be to create, grow, and maintain the product as a sustainable business looking to operate side by side with other industry competition. Another strategy is to create a product, demonstrate proof of concept, and sell the product to a larger company for profit. A business owner may create a product and offer a strategic partnership to grow both brands as a business strategy. The strategy of the concept will also determine concept creation. The strategy will speak to decisions concerning financial resources, time constraints, and data collection. The business model will be the mechanism to accomplish the strategy. The business model and the business strategy are intertwined to maximize the opportunity for market entry. The business model creates the strategy, and in some cases, the strategy creates the model. If the entrepreneur has developed a strategy for the innovation in advance and has assessed the model needed to execute the strategy, then the resources are the following guidelines for execution. However, it is common for the strategy to develop out of necessity and available resources. Some of the variables to consider when comparing the business model and the business strategy are as follows in Table 3.1.

Table 3.1 Variables and parameters for business models and strategy

Variables for a business model and business strategy	Parameters for a business strategy
Customer value proposition	Business model
Customer segments and distribution channels	External environment
Primary and support activities	Internal environment
Key resource and partners	Position
Competence	Action plan
Revenue streams and cost structure	Attitude toward execution

Source: Štefan and Branislav (2016).

During the strategic brainstorm of the concept creation process, there are detailed aspects to consider. The environmental quality resulting from the human action, diagnose the baseline condition, compare the impact of various scenarios, reduce the amount of complex information in decision-making, and instrumentalize the monitoring phase to determine progress (Mata-Lima et al. 2016). These actions will provide a roadmap for comparison and allow for observance of errors and oversights to during the concept creation phase. A conceptual framework is created to remind the business owner of the purpose and opportunity while going through the creative process where the original direction and plan can quickly be forgotten or misdirected.

Case Study: Two Supply and Facility Companies

Company A: A Training Facility and Platform

A company was created (company name withheld) to provide physical training for people looking to receive specialized training in various methods at any given time during the day or night for convenience. The training facility was known concept heavily flooded in the industry. The dream was to create a platform offering training in a proprietary method to capitalize on travel schedules, unique talents, and ever-changing goals. There was no doubt the proprietary training method was a radical innovation driven by purpose, with a recognized opportunity. Company A was going to provide a place for clients to train while also supplying the proprietary model for a continued interaction touch point. There was a considerable outline of the business strategy which provided Company A with the belief they would have a significant strategic advantage over the competition. The issue with the concept was the lack of meta-cognition surrounding stakeholder collaboration and a suitable business model. The customer stakeholder and the entrepreneur were served well in the innovation; however, the distribution and human capital stakeholders needed to power the concept were left wanting. The business model was also not conducive for mass distribution, awareness, or a legitimate monetization scale. As a result of these reasons Company A was not able to make a successful market entry without a substantial financial contribution unrealistic for the conceptual stage.

Company B: NeXgen Vapors®

NeXgen Vapors® is a retail vapor shop with a host of proprietary flavored vapors. The retail shop boasts a consistent clientele with over four years of existence. The dream of the owner was not only to own and run a vapor store but also to create a laboratory with the ability to supply FDA approved and regulated flavors only produced by NeXgen Vapors®. From the onset of the creation of the company, there was a substantial purpose and opportunity outline. The incremental innovation became a radical innovation when the FDA placed regulations on the number of new flavors allowed to enter into the market. NeXgen Vapors® had introduced and gain clearance for roughly 200 proprietary flavors unable to be legally duplicated in any format. This reality led to a fully equipped laboratory with the ability to scale nationally to provide distribution for exponential growth. The concept born out of changes in the industry, entrepreneur knowledge, and market analysis. The business model and the business strategy demonstrated a good fit as all of the stakeholders benefited from the innovation provided by NeXgen Vapors®.

Figure 3.1 NeXgen vapors® New logo and legal authorization to distribute

Figure 3.2 NeXgen vapors® retail store

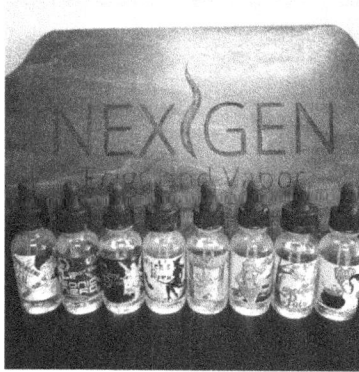

Figure 3.3 NeXgen vapors® flavor proprietary flavor samples

Chapter 3 Review:
Concept Creation—Defining the Dream

1. Take the time to define the concept and the type of concept created accurately

2. Image Builder, Strategic Transformer, Reactive Defender or Performance Enhancer

3. The product, process, and organizational innovation are three types of innovation
4. Innovation can be radical or incremental
5. The creation of a concept must benefit all stakeholders
6. The business model and business strategy must accompany the concept

CHAPTER 4

Viability Report— Feasibility Study

The first three chapters covered the thoughts and mental position of the entrepreneur. The purpose of the concept, product, or service connects with the passion and the rationale for market entry. Recognizing the opportunity speaks to the ability to acknowledge demands in the market along with timing for entry. The concept creation stage is the image building and brand value proposition for the entrepreneur or small business owner. The viability report and feasibility study combine the thoughts and mental position of the entrepreneur with information and data for appropriate decision-making. Working through the business model and the business strategy becomes more clear during this stage as concrete realities are made known.

Purpose of the Viability Report and Feasibility Study

The viability report and feasibility study are different from a business plan. Many entrepreneurs are familiar with the notion of a business plan whether they are proficient in writing one or acknowledge the need for one. A business plan does not denote if a concept, product, or service is feasible for entry or viable for the long term. The latter two aspects are crucial for business survival. Feasibility studies reduce the risk in product launches, reassuring the entrepreneur, small business owners, investors, and other pertinent stakeholders on the potential of wasted cost (Morgan, Hejdenberg, Hinrichs-Krapels, and Armstrong 2018). Immediate action without understanding leads to entry issues for the entrepreneur as mistakes are made in placement, design, utility concerning stakeholder expectation. Entrepreneurs committing to the first promising route of entry based on emotion, passions, and eagerness leave their concept vulnerable to competitors, financial errors, and marketplace misplacement (Gans, Scott, and Stern 2018). A weak entry plan will set the occasion for competitors to exploit weaknesses in the entry and leverage those weaknesses for their gain. Exploitation exists in the form of enhancing the concept and removing the advantage of the entrepreneur. Other forms of exploitation exist in the method of cease and desist actions from unknown infringements and inadequate protection. Every action taken by the entrepreneur will cost money and need economic resources to navigate. The frivolous action causes increased spending through wasteful trial and error. Improper product placement upon entry creates confusion in the market to the point where consumers are unsure of how to appreciate or interact with the concept, service, or product. All of these aspects are dangerous for the sustainability goals of the entrepreneur or small business owner.

Creating a business or launching a new product is a complex activity due to the number of obstacles inherent in the process. Viability reports and feasibility studies prepare the entrepreneur and small business owner for known barriers. Entrepreneurs who plan are more likely to create a more viable venture and are better equipped for flexibility and responsive action (Greene and Hopp 2018). The viability report and feasibility study are not to guarantee success in the marketplace but to provide an outline of widespread expectations for navigation. The reports and study appear novel to new entrepreneurs, but people informally conduct a feasibility study and viability report in their daily lives. When a family chooses to go on vacation, they automatically begin researching the weather conditions, travel accommodations, available activities, associated costs, appropriate apparel, and corresponding dates. Some families formally chart this information and heavily plan while others think about these aspects and pack accordingly. There are many variables through the course of the vacation that may change the experience for the family such as unexpected rain, activity shut-downs, or delays in travel, however, the mental exercise of viability and feasibility prepares the family for the unforeseen events more than the unprepared family. This reality is the same for entrepreneurs and small business owners in their quest to launch new concepts, products, and services. On average, the most successful entrepreneurs who generate viability studies and feasibility studies increase the probability of sustainability (Greene and Hopp 2018). This step allows for the entrepreneur to

become more familiar with their industry, market, and the value proposition of the product.

The viability report and feasibility study remove the emotion from the
launch of a concept, product, or service and provide objectionable measures. Positive emotions pose dangers to entrepreneurs and small business
owners due to feeling overoptimistic about their innovation leading to the
overemphasis of potential benefits, returns on investments, and market
share capture (Healey and Hodgkinson 2017). This energetic feel leads
to misinterpretations and oversights of fundamental truths in the market
paramount for long-term success. From a creative standpoint, innovation is exciting and inspiring. The challenge is looking at the innovation
from a practical and tangible standpoint to provide balance in observation. The feasibility study and viability report bring legitimacy when
acknowledging an opportunity and executing the delivery. Small business
owners and entrepreneurs benefit from strategic planning coordinating
different implementation techniques formalized through the feasibility
study and viability reporting activities (Barraket, Furneaux, Barth, and
Mason 2016). The reporting and study exercises keep the entrepreneur
focused on realities affecting their opportunities in a real way. Combining
the creative process with a formal research process promotes a holistic
approach for successful market entry.

Strength of Viability Report and Feasibility Study

The timing of the launch is as essential to the success of a launch as any
other factor. When innovation occurs, thoughts begin to surround speed
of development and the competitive advantage of quick entry. These
thoughts eliminate the need for a comprehensive viability report and
feasibility study. The entrepreneur should be aware of this perception
as many errors abound with this logic. Small business owners operate
with increased layers of uncertainty and worry surrounding the belief
exploration and research will delay commercialization causing execution
of the first available strategy deriding the deliberation and planning stage
(Gans et al. 2018). A common belief is time is equivalent to money. The
time spent developing and introducing a product in the market can be
judged based on overall efficiency and productivity. Getting to market

quicker and earning income can arrive at the expense of sustainability and higher income potential. Saving time, energy, and resources generated from careful analysis at the onset of concept creation. For a launch to be effective, the detail of the opportunity, customer profile, company operation, and breakdown of the needed resources are prudent research steps (Greene and Hopp 2018). Understanding these areas will prevent time wasting activities or misjudgment in the market.

The entrepreneur and small business will have an idea of what accomplishment is desired with the innovation but is not privy to all of the factors affecting the performance of the new concept, product, or service. Complex matters and interdependence make decision-making and market understanding difficult for start-ups. The choice of customers influences, the organizational identity, technological options, and other industry threats create a myriad of complexities for the entrepreneur and small business owner (Gans et al. 2018). The concept creation stage is the period the viability report, and feasibility study needs to be completed. Conducting the report and study during this time will increase the knowledge of entry and determine mediating factors for the entrepreneur. The strength of the viability report and feasibility study is to inform of the effectiveness of the activity through the analysis of factors in both the process and product leading to increased symbolic legitimacy (Barraket et al. 2016). Taking the time to go through the process of viability report and feasibility study provides a foundation of informational certainty to operate. The dimensions of research also provide superior performance as opposed to guesswork along with trial and error. The strategic orientation during the study and reporting phase create the proper behavior in both innovation and market analysis leading to a positive effect on the company's performance (Ogbari et al. 2018). The symbolic legitimacy and the positive effect on performance increase the emotional consideration surrounding strategy and future execution breeding more confidence for the entrepreneur. How small business owners react to opportunities and threats arise from the information derived from the collection of information, preparation, and anticipation of obstacles by the entrepreneur and small business owner (Healey and Hodgkinson 2017). Formulating critical thinking opportunities and meta-cognition before launch in a formal way is an excellent exercise to increase the opportunity for success for the product or service launch.

Decision-making and Success

Viability reports and feasibility studies are not the guarantees of success for any company or entrepreneur. The report and the study are not created to guarantee success but outlining known variables for decision-making. An assumption of the start-up process is the data extracted from the analysis of business plans and reports directly lead to high-level success and the elimination of all uncertainty (Schramm 2018). The created reports and studies work in conjunction with action, stakeholder collaboration, and concentration on execution. Decision-making is the residual from the knowledge gathered and the goals sought. Viability reports and feasibility studies directly assist decision-making and high-risk choice options. Emotions connect to a decision when information and energy are surrounding a proposed alternative, especially when the probability and utility of another option are insufficient to compel bold choices and challenge convictions (Healey and Hodgkinson 2017). Entrepreneurs and small business owners leaning on minimal information demonstrate the inability to exhibit the decision-making necessary for a successful launch. The challenge of a more robust report and study provide a more extensive range of scenarios preparing the entrepreneur for more successful avenues during the market entry stage. The sake of futurity comes from careful observation reducing riskiness. Possible future occurrences are directly related to the entrepreneur decision-making process which reflects knowledge of sales forecasts, possible industry changes, alterations in customer preference, and tracking environmental changes (Ogbari et al. 2018). Gathering knowledge ahead of time on meaningful and significant industry factors are beneficial for a successful product or service launch.

Components of the Viability
Report and Feasibility Study

There are no concrete methods for writing viability reports and feasibility studies. These activities exist as a framework for entry and not as a universal method delivering entry success. The more information collected and perspectives analyzed the more varied and diverse the opportunity for success. Founders are more confident, persuasive to investors, and consumers when demonstrating ideas across multiple strategies while validating underlying assumptions and strengths of the innovation (Gans et al. 2018). All of the stakeholders account for in the development of the concept and a comprehensive viability report, and feasibility study will offer this. To maintain control of the innovation and find a way to provide value in the existing marketplace the intellectual property, value chain, and disruptive properties are all considered in execution (Gans et al. 2018). Control of the innovation allows for the entrepreneur or small business owner to remain focused on the tangible deliveries for maintaining a schedule and cost responsibility.

The viability report and feasibility study comprehensively break down various aspects needed for a good product launch. The following topics are foundational components of a viability report and feasibility study

Description: The description of the product is detailed and specific. A thorough explanation of the utility and design of the concept, product, or service will allow all stakeholders to understand the innovation appropriately. As mentioned previously, the understanding and interaction with the concept, product, or service is a major determining factor for successful market entry and sustainability.

Core Industry: An appropriate diagnosis for market entry extends from outlining the core industry. The previous success and failures in the industry provide insight on how to navigate with the innovation. Analysis of the industry carves a right path for product placement in the market. Researching reactions to the other concepts, products, or services increases the knowledge of consumer behavior invaluable to the entrepreneur.

Trends, Substitutes, Complements: The trends, substitutes, and complements are paramount for recognizing competition and opportunity. Like products, industry-altering products, and connecting products are discovered at a higher level during this stage. Trends allow the entrepreneur to determine how the market is changing, shifting, or behaving. If a concept, product, or service is out of trend, then the likelihood of success is low. For instance, the trend in the current climate is the Internet-of-things for connectivity.

If an entrepreneur's concept, product, or service is based on analog solutions, the novelty for market entry is reduced. Substitutes for a concept, product, or service are hazardous to the longevity and sustainability opportunities. An example of a substitute is a vegetarian burger over a beef hamburger. If the trend in the food and beverage industry heavily slants toward perceived healthier options, the introduction of a new beef hamburger restaurant may be thwarted by an organic cafe serving black bean burgers. Beverage companies experience this reality with flavored waters substituting sugary drinks. Complements are other concepts, products, and services providing an increase for the new concept, product, or service. An instance of a complement is the reality of mustard and ketchup sales having an attachment to hamburgers and hot dog sales. If the fluctuation of one or the other rises or decreases, the impact is experienced by the other product immediately. Every concept, product, or service must know where the complements lie to anticipate indirect rises and falls.

Market Need: Discovering the needs in the market is a sure way of providing value to the market. Consumers will display direct behavior and indirect signs on where the advantage exists for the entrepreneur. The key is not to ignore the signs and the behavior of the consumer as they will lead to successful entry. Needs will manifest in many ways and will also disguise as wants. Regarding commercialization and monetization, the wants of the consumer are translated into needs as well. Satisfying the wants of people becomes a solution worth paying for which leads to a successful product launch.

Competitive Landscape: Paying close attention to the current competition allows for the concept, product, or service differentiation. The slightest change or alteration to a product or service will change the interaction and perception of the consumer providing a competitive edge. In other cases, finding a unique difference in a concept, product, or service is not essential due to market size. Uber® and Lyft® provide the same service without significant recognition differences in their service. McDonald's®, Burger King®, and Big Boy® all serve a sandwich with similar ingredients. McDonald's®

Big Mac®, Burger King's® Big King®, and Big Boy's® Big Boy Sandwich® are mostly the same sandwich but serve such a large market; each product can experience success. The viability report and feasibility study will help the entrepreneur have an awareness of these realities with their product.

Management Team: Long-term success of any company resides with the team charged with execution. The skills and collective experience of the team will propel the entry or pull down the momentum. The team does not have to be a large group of members but a qualified group of members for the benefit of the stakeholders. Entrepreneurs and start-up founders may only have two or three members assisting them in their quest. Proper placement of these members will make the difference in a successful launch or increased issues slowing the process. Confidence for achieving product launch success derives from knowledge and team ability. Analysis of their skills of each member is a benefit when embarking on a product launch.

Financials: The financial and economic resources needed to enter a market successfully may not be completely available from the onset. The research will indicate how much money is needed to perform the entry with the understanding unforeseeable aspects always appear. The viability report and feasibility study will highlight many of the initial costs to construct a prudent budget. Once the preliminary budget generates, the research will assist with creating a number providing a financial cushion offsetting increased expenses. This vital step provides an in-depth look at the longevity projections for decision-making.

Regulation: A very intricate aspect of concept creation is the acknowledgment and adherence to laws, certifications, regulations, licenses, and compliance. Many founders fail due to improper guideline compliance and regulatory infractions. Concepts, products, and services bound by laws, licenses, and other regulatory bodies must take the time to align with mandates properly. Shortcuts in this realm not only can cause failure but excessive fines and even incarceration. The excuse of ignorance is not an appropriate defense for infringements and violations.

The responsibility is incumbent on the founder to operate in an ethical, legal, and compliant manner.

Qualitative Analysis: Entrepreneurs and small business owners are susceptible to emotional connections to innovation. The opinions of stakeholders, case studies, and field research assists in providing invaluable feedback on the receptivity of the concept, product, or service. Interviewing consumers, beta testing, and questionnaires are ways to conduct a qualitative analysis providing genuine and authentic feedback for a better understanding of the fit in the market. Ignoring or preceding this step forces the entrepreneur to lean on personal views and beliefs which may not reflect the views and opinions of the target audience.

SWOT Analysis: The word SWOT is a commonly used acronym for strengths, weaknesses, opportunities, and threats. The SWOT analysis is quick and straightforward providing a snapshot of the concept, product, or service. The strength is the aspect of connecting confidence and purpose to the market entry. The weakness is the aspect that has does not have a known solution. This weakness may or may not preclude a successful market entry. The opportunity is the reason for optimism for the market entry. The threats are those competitors and substitutes presenting themselves as a barrier to entry or growth. All of the aspects of the SWOT analysis should be considered and well known.

Case Study: Two New Start-Ups

Company A: An Entertainment Company

A company was created (company name withheld) to provide family entertainment for a particular region in the Midwest. This company took over the operation from another entity only in existence for one year. During the partial year, the company lost nearly $30,000 in revenue. After seeking assistance, the company was optimistic about their ability to run the company as opposed to the previous owners. This new ownership had never owned a company before but was confident because of their experience in the corporate setting. One of the owners was an accountant by trade, and the other owner was a private banker. The skill set of the owners did not correlate the activities or skill set needed for the entertainment company. Pure enthusiasm for the type of entertainment and the perceived family need, led the owners to believe ownership would be an instant success. The difficulty of ownership was realized through the significant financial losses. A viability report and feasibility study concluded the losses would continue to abound. Based on the industry, the region, and current consumer behavior, the owners would lose an additional $100,000 in revenue, even if their operation was perfect. This analysis conducted best case scenarios, qualitative analysis, and trend research. The owners would have benefited from a viability report and feasibility study from the onset before embarking on the venture.

Company B: SPI Products® The Alum Clock©

The company SPI Products® created a product entitled the Alum Clock© which is a dual function granite clock with a matching paperweight/coaster combo. The formation of the company surrounded the intellectual property, The Alum Clock©. The owners carried the belief a uniquely made clock was a novel concept especially with the addition of an institution name or school mascot attached. This imagery would connect to graduates, creating nostalgia, and inspiring them to purchase hence the name "Alum Clock©." The viability report and feasibility revealed the watch and clock market was a $9.4 billion industry. The awards and recognition market stood at $94 billion, while the home decor market was a $664 billion market. The report and study changed the course of direction for market entry for the owner allowing a better market entry position along with greater strategic partners providing useful short-cuts in licensing, manufacturing, and product placement. The report and study were able to save time and increase finances to proper product placement and a better understanding of how to serve the market.

Figure 4.1 SPI Products® and Alum Clock© products and site

Chapter 4 Review: Viability Report and Feasibility Study

1. Viability reports and feasibility studies prepare for known barriers
2. Reduces risk
3. Enhances decision-making
4. Increases percentages for success
5. Components are:
   (a) Description
   (b) Core industry
   (c) Trends, substitutes, complements
   (d) Market need
   (e) Competitive landscape
   (f) Management team
   (g) Financials
   (h) Regulation
   (i) Qualitative analysis
   (j) SWOT analysis

CHAPTER 5

Value Proposition

The preceding chapters focused on the fundamental steps of understanding a new concept, product, or service in preparation for a successful launch. This chapter focuses on the consumer through perception and the company value proposition. As learned in the viability report and feasibility study section, the approach to the market for the entrepreneur and small business owner can be very different from the trend of the market; the same is said for the consumer value proposition. Defining or having an idea of the value proposition is a conscious and essential action for the entrepreneur. Understanding value is not a primary or straightforward task. Many small business owners and founders define value as low cost, exceptional service, or high-quality products which are only a fragment of what value encompasses in the mind of the consumer (Lecours 2017). Entrepreneurs benefit from taking the time to analyze potential value propositions for consumers. Many entrepreneurs, start-ups, and small business owners are not proficient at creating a value proposition for consumers. Communicating customer value propositions in a way to help customers make firm assessments are difficult challenges due to a lack of knowledge of how to offer the innovation, determining the resources to support the innovation, and how to position the innovation (Wouters, Anderson, and Kirchberger 2018). Developing a consciousness on how to illustrate the value proposition will be vital in getting to market successfully.

How to Create Value for Consumers

Consumer value propositions are not directly defined and are fluid in interpretation. As a result of this reality, entrepreneurs struggle with concretely integrating the value proposition during the market entry phase. Contextually and inherently consumer values vary due to reasons such as experience, desires, exposure, and access making it difficult for small business owners and entrepreneurs to develop a solid value proposition (Rintamäki and Kirves 2017). Instead of looking to narrow down the value for each consumer group accurately, entrepreneurs succeed by focusing on broader and all-encompassing strategies. Creating solutions to benefit the targeted consumer base adds value. The focus on consumers' productivity, behavior, and operations develop the capability of sensing needs and requests from the consumers for value creation (Riihimäki, Kaartemo, and Zettinig 2016). Instances for benefiting consumers become evident in the viability report and feasibility study. Careful consideration of the extracted information through qualitative analysis and case studies provide valuable consumer opinions.

The context of consumer response amplifies the strategic differentiation by making dimensions of consumer value more relevant than others (Rintamäki and Kirves 2017). Innovation ranks in priority due to the ever-changing needs of the consumer. Viewing the needs in priority of consumer importance is the best way to provide perceived value among the consumer market. For instance, a new product may enhance the interaction of the consumer with a grocery store. If the innovation speeds up the process of grocery shopping by 30 percent but raises the cost of groceries by 120 percent, the innovation does not exist as a value proposition for the consumer in context. It is conceivable many consumers will opt for longer wait times to save the additional money related to grocery shopping. Entrepreneurs may ignore explicit consumer value propositions for many reasons. Common beliefs of novelty in concept development creates an automatic need in the market blinding the small business owner from concentrating on authentic value propositions compounded by insufficient understanding of how innovations holistically affect consumers lead to ignoring consumer value (Wouters et al. 2018). These errors set the occasion for market mismatch and failed product launches. The actual manifestation of an entrepreneur or small business' commitment to the consumer market is through a strategic value focus. According to Biloshapka and Osiyevskyy (2018) questions such as these three lead to the discovery of a consumer value proposition :

1. How do you make sure you are offering the benefits your customers appreciate most?

2. What group of customers is the primary focus of your efforts?

3. How do you help your customers fully appreciate the delivery of the benefits offered?

How to Recognize the Value Proposition

Understanding and recognizing the appropriate value proposition for the consumer market is paramount for product sustainability. Recognition can be immediate and intentional while at other times the recognition can manifest accidentally. The earliest form of detection derives from the mental and emotional position of the entrepreneur. The founder, start-up, or small business owner has to be authentic and genuine in the approach of solutions or providing options for the consumer. Research has alluded to the desirability of an authentic brand position regarding delivering value to consumers achieving self-authentication and perceived connectivity (Napoli, Dickinson-Delaporte, and Beverland 2016). Listening to the consumer base through qualitative studies and market research allow for the business owner or entrepreneur to create products proving legitimate value to the consumer. Affinity for the concept, product, or service develops from a pure value realized value proposition. There are two value propositions realized by consumers. The innovative offering value proposition communicates how the innovation provides superior merit for problem-solving or achieving top consumer priority; while the leveraging assistance value proposition conveys what the consumer will get in return for supporting the concept, product or service (Wouters et al. 2018). Value is recognized by making consumers life more comfortable, better, or more enjoyable. The innovative offering introduces something new for the consumer to enhance life or solves problems. The leveraging assistance value proposition highlights what makes the offering worthwhile and worthy of attention. An entrepreneur cannot be company-facing when looking to engage the consumer market through value propositioning. The focus is on entry success come from acknowledgment and acceptance from the consumer market.

Developing a method for identification of value proposition has a multilayered complexity when considering execution but is simple as an overall concept. Understanding what customers value is a precondition for formulating competitive consumer value by investigating the assessment of the tradeoff between benefits and sacrifices enabled by consumer perception (Rintamäki and Kirves 2017). Consumers will make judgments about the entrepreneur or small business owner offering and determine if the concept, product, or service is worth the effort or the money. This reality is not new or revolutionary. Every person is a consumer of some product or service including entrepreneurs, founders, and small business owners. The error many entrepreneurs make is looking at the innovation from a sensationalized perspective as opposed to a practical and universal perspective. The simplicity in determining a reasonable value proposition is thinking of the benefit to the consumer allowing the consumer to participate in a real and straightforward manner. Confusing or costly concepts will dramatically affect the consumer value proposition and product launch. Consumer-derived and brand derived value are attributed to authentic positioning related to the familiarity of branding or consumer needs (Napoli et al. 2016). The term authentic is continuously used to emphasize the focus on the need of the consumer more than the need of the company. This focus is internalized by the consumer leading to a higher probability of success during market entry. Seeing the reflection of the consumer is an essential part of measuring the value proposition for the entrepreneur to determine development, integration, and delivery.

Delivery of Value to the Consumer

Once the entrepreneur identifies the value proposition, the challenge is delivering the proposition to the consumer. The delivery takes place through communication and development. To manage the customer value proposition, the entrepreneur has to measure and model the innovation in a relevant context for the benefit of the stakeholders (Rintamäki and Kirves 2017). The viability report and feasibility study phase offer the opportunity to gain feedback and information through qualitative analysis. This stage will also carve out the path for value delivery to the consumer. The value proposition lies within the confines of the brand recognition or path of access. If the consumer does not recognize the concept, product, or service they will not interact or value the offering.

The same is to be said if the concept, product, or service cannot quickly reach the intended audience. The goal for the innovation is to resonate with the targeted audience in a meaningful. A resonating focus is formulated relative to the consumer's next-best alternative and includes favorable points of difference pinpointing top priorities and concerns (Wouters et al. 2018). An example of resonating with consumers is through the use of gathering feedback and measuring connectivity through interaction. This reality happens in many ways in the current climate. Social media, referral, and repeat interaction are ways to determine if the value resonates as a value proposition for consumers. The value proposition can be learned by delivering the entrepreneur's innovation or examining the competition in the marketplace. Consumers negotiate meaning with different cues to identify elements of a genuine consumption experience (Napoli et al. 2016). Through the delivery of the innovation, the cues provided by the consumer market will detail how the entrepreneur should continue to navigate the product launch or make adjustments. The consumer market will validate the innovation and provide early adoption in the initial phases if offered before the product launch. This validation gives the entrepreneur confidence the innovation provides meaningful value to the consumer for acceptance.

Case Study: Two Tech Solution Companies

Company A: A Tech Solution Company

A company was created (company name withheld) to provide a tech solution for businesses and entertainers to increase visibility and commercial opportunity. The concept was to become a start-up headed by a very successful business owner whose family had a history of creating successful companies. The business owner and the family made millions in retail and manufacturing over decades but had never owned a company involved in technology. The concept was established by the actions and interactions of other business owners and celebrity entertainers. Based on the private and collective conversations the notion of creating a technological solution to engage both parties became the remedy. The owners displayed passion, purpose, and a plan for execution. The issue became apparent

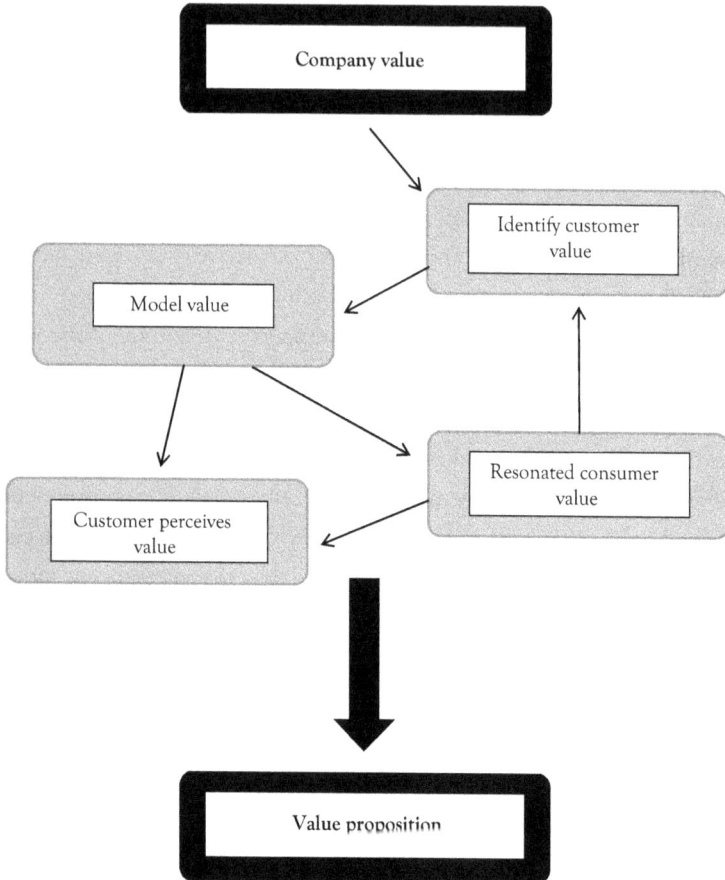

Figure 5.1 Cycle of consumer value

when the question was posed about monetization and scalability. Weeks of meta-cognition, meetings, and collaboration could not unveil a value proposition worthy enough for consumer engagement. The end-user and "who" stood to benefit most from the innovation was unclear. The business owners remained enthusiast about the potential of success the technology would provide but never could determine how the technology could be delivered in a precise and reasonably priced method. Increased scrutiny surrounding the technology decreases the value of the technology. This reality ultimately stopped the technology from moving forward for market entry.

Company B: SkinnyOffice©

The company TierFive® provides enterprise-class IT solutions at a price small businesses can afford and budget. The solutions exist to specifically help small business owners overcome the hurdle of upfront capital expenses associated with growing the company's IT needs. The value to the consumer is having a comprehensive IT solution allowing business owners the peace of mind to focus on the task of running the business efficiently. The services consist of security, voice, electronic fax, managed IT infrastructure, fiber, disaster recovery, and virtual data. The innovation

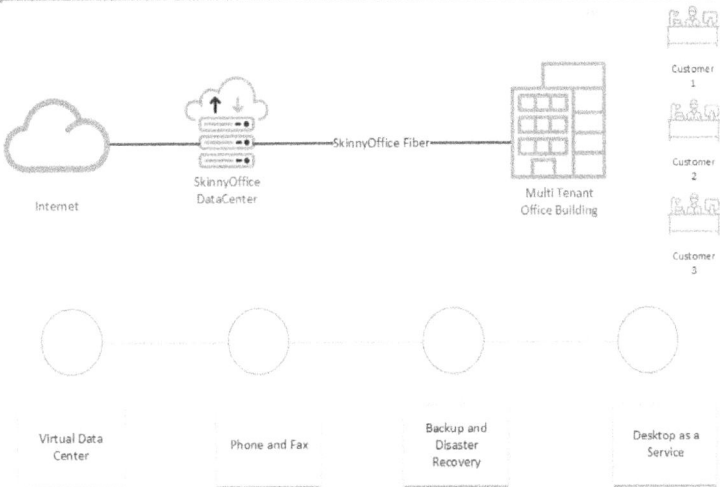

Figure 5.2 SkinnyOffice© design and services

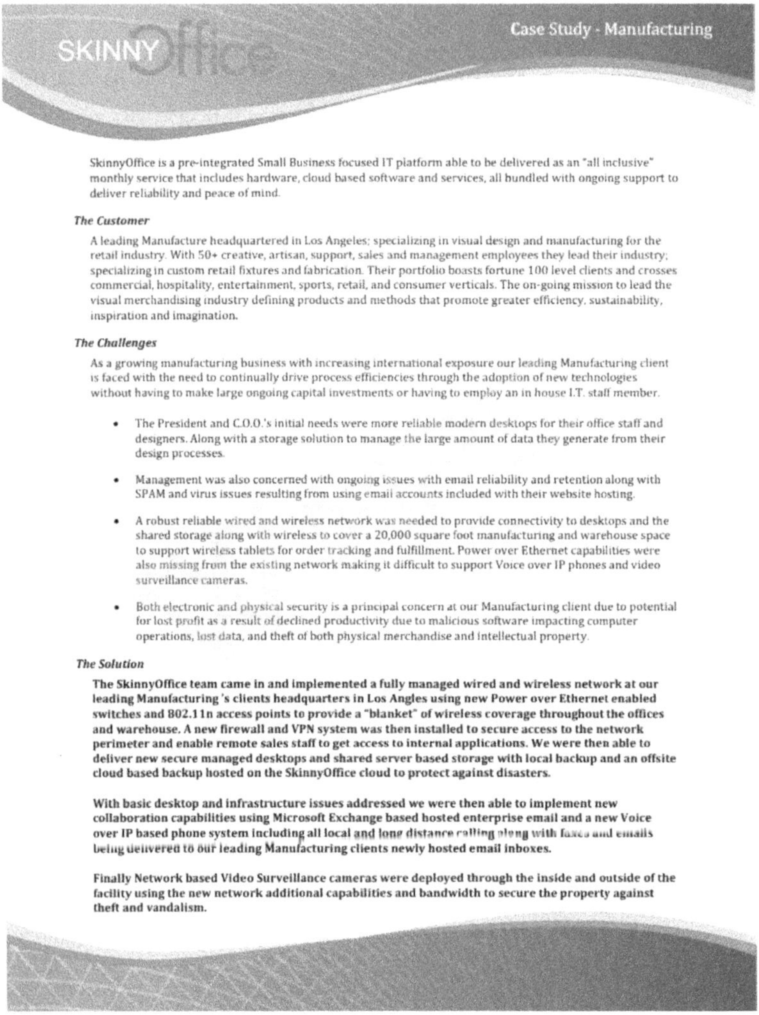

SKINNY Office

Case Study - Manufacturing

SkinnyOffice is a pre-integrated Small Business focused IT platform able to be delivered as an "all inclusive" monthly service that includes hardware, cloud based software and services, all bundled with ongoing support to deliver reliability and peace of mind.

The Customer

A leading Manufacture headquartered in Los Angeles; specializing in visual design and manufacturing for the retail industry. With 50+ creative, artisan, support, sales and management employees they lead their industry; specializing in custom retail fixtures and fabrication. Their portfolio boasts fortune 100 level clients and crosses commercial, hospitality, entertainment, sports, retail, and consumer verticals. The on-going mission to lead the visual merchandising industry defining products and methods that promote greater efficiency, sustainability, inspiration and imagination.

The Challenges

As a growing manufacturing business with increasing international exposure our leading Manufacturing client is faced with the need to continually drive process efficiencies through the adoption of new technologies without having to make large ongoing capital investments or having to employ an in house I.T. staff member.

- The President and C.O.O.'s initial needs were more reliable modern desktops for their office staff and designers. Along with a storage solution to manage the large amount of data they generate from their design processes.
- Management was also concerned with ongoing issues with email reliability and retention along with SPAM and virus issues resulting from using email accounts included with their website hosting.
- A robust reliable wired and wireless network was needed to provide connectivity to desktops and the shared storage along with wireless to cover a 20,000 square foot manufacturing and warehouse space to support wireless tablets for order tracking and fulfillment. Power over Ethernet capabilities were also missing from the existing network making it difficult to support Voice over IP phones and video surveillance cameras.
- Both electronic and physical security is a principal concern at our Manufacturing client due to potential for lost profit as a result of declined productivity due to malicious software impacting computer operations, lost data, and theft of both physical merchandise and intellectual property.

The Solution

The SkinnyOffice team came in and implemented a fully managed wired and wireless network at our leading Manufacturing 's clients headquarters in Los Angles using new Power over Ethernet enabled switches and 802.11n access points to provide a "blanket" of wireless coverage throughout the offices and warehouse. A new firewall and VPN system was then installed to secure access to the network perimeter and enable remote sales staff to get access to internal applications. We were then able to deliver new secure managed desktops and shared server based storage with local backup and an offsite cloud based backup hosted on the SkinnyOffice cloud to protect against disasters.

With basic desktop and infrastructure issues addressed we were then able to implement new collaboration capabilities using Microsoft Exchange based hosted enterprise email and a new Voice over IP based phone system including all local and long distance calling along with faxes and emails being delivered to our leading Manufacturing clients newly hosted email inboxes.

Finally Network based Video Surveillance cameras were deployed through the inside and outside of the facility using the new network additional capabilities and bandwidth to secure the property against theft and vandalism.

Figure 5.3 SkinnyOffice© value proposition to consumer

of SkinnyOffice demonstrates value in the consumer marketplace by solving complex IT issues, recognizably, with an affordable cost for the small business sector. Years in the IT sector validated the concept creation of SkinnyOffice allowing for a successful entry with growth opportunity.

Chapter 5 Review: Value Proposition

1. Create solutions benefiting the consumer
2. Innovative value offering and leveraging assistance value offering are two ways to recognize the value
3. Confusing or costly concepts negatively affect consumer value
4. Consumer-derived and brand-derived value attribute to authentic positioning
5. Path of the delivery lead to the consumer value recognition
6. The consumer market will validate the value proposition providing confidence to the entrepreneur

CHAPTER 6

Team Building for Execution

The introduction of innovation into the consumer market begins with a concept, extends to research, and ultimately ends with development. The foundation of product development is vital for sustainability. The knowledge and information acquired during the viability report and feasibility study are critical for short-term and long-term decision-making. The entrepreneur or start-up founder consciousness and awareness regarding team-member selection is equally as important as the foundational research. A poorly selected team prevents a good product from market entry while a good team increases the opportunity for a successful launch. In the entrepreneur space, the team can be employees, contracted workers, investors, or partners. High performing teams result when groups of people share common beliefs, principles, or values (Ruygrok 2016). The agreement between the members of the organization will bode well for all of the stakeholders affected by the innovation. Extended the shared beliefs and values beyond monetary success benefits the entrepreneur, founder of the start-up, and small business owner considering limited financial resources and slow return on investment cycles.

Defining a Team

The first order of business for an entrepreneur is to define the team needed to conduct a successful market entry launch. Particular characteristics, skills, knowledge, and the social network theory contribute to the selection of team members for a small business or start-up (Forsström-Tuominen, Jussila, and Goel 2017). The characteristics. skills, and knowledge of each member determine what role the member occupies. An entrepreneurial team is defined as two or more people jointly developing and establishing a business with common goals and outcomes (Forsström-Tuominen, Jussila, and Goel 2017). This unit is responsible for the action of conducting the research, providing insight, and performing the work on the concept or product. Essential functions to achieve maximum results for the team are communication and collaboration. Open communication and active collaboration yield a cohesion forming the three "C's" of team-building (Lejeck 2017). The action of the communication, collaboration, and cohesion bring the members closer in the workflow to leverage the strengths of each member. The combination of communication, collaboration, and cohesion create the company culture. The culture is the set of norms driving the behavior and performance of the company (Ruygrok 2016). The entrepreneur operates as the sum of the members of the organization pushing to the market and launch the innovation. The real value of teamwork and collaboration lies in the ability to draw from diverse experiences, varying perspectives, and different contextual clues to accomplish organizational goals along with consumer problems (Thayer, Petruzzelli, and McClurg 2018). When member's perspective resonates with the appointed leader, confidence ensues among the members. People respond better to inclusion, information sharing, and responsibility (Barden 2018).

The unique abilities of the individuals create the strength of the collective group. Building a team does not denote a large team with unlimited resources. Each member of the team can be responsible for a host of activity. Every member benefits from the empowerment provided by the entrepreneur or small business owner. Members will make errors, engage in controversial thinking, and seek outside learning opportunities during the innovation development stages (Harvey 2016). The reality of these perceived issues are the dynamic and ever-changing industries and consumer markets. Entrepreneurial teams succeed when the mentality gears toward flexibility and change. The varying opinions and perceptions assist the entrepreneur in recognizing areas of opportunity or avoiding barriers in the industry.

Characteristics of an Entrepreneur Team

Building a team for a start-up or a small business is must different than building for a large company. Individual-level attributes, dispositions, and behaviors can influence outcomes at different layers of a company

(Thayer et al. 2018). Diversity and member cognition play a significant part in the overall success of concept creation. Entrepreneurs and founders must associate and partner with other members boasting high functioning and valuable skill to the organization. This group of member's agility and expertise will determine an adequate product launch with the ability to adjust to meet consumer needs throughout the phases of development and entry (Barden 2018). This agile team is made up of a few members or a large team. Common positions needed to bring a product, service, or a concept to market is:

- Entrepreneur/Founder
- Operations
- Chief Financial Officer
- Chief Technical Officer
- Business Development
- Commercial Development
- Marketing and Advertising
- Legal
- Investors
- Performers/Assistants

All of these members may not sit in a position commanding immediate compensation. It is common for one or two people to fulfill many of the roles represented. Role switching typically happens due to limited finances, a smaller network, or the neglect of a position. When a start-up can fill these positions with members of the desired culture, the higher the development work. An entrepreneur simultaneously fulfilling these roles is subject to burnout or poor execution. Breakdowns in any one of these roles or functions will decrease the opportunity for success dramatically. Marketing and development efforts lead to product awareness among the target audience. Developing a product no one hears about is not a successful execution strategy. Consequently, the investors and legal team provide the necessary finances and protection for sustainability. The technological needs are essential to how the consumers experience the innovation. The role of the team is crucial for an appropriate product launch. Entrepreneurs must be purposeful and deliberate with the team-building efforts.

Case Study: A Home Improvement Company

An aspiring entrepreneur inquired about creating a home improvement company with a novel method to beautify homes. The entrepreneur posed grand ideas regarding launch and the expected consumer receptivity. The entrepreneur wrote a business plan and could demonstrate a reasonable consumer value proposition. The most significant barrier to the journey is the lack of a team. The idea for the company called for maintenance, building, transporting, ordering, business development, and a substantial capital contribution or investment. The entrepreneur did not have anyone to alleviate the responsibility of any of the roles connected to proper market entry. The innovation never made it to market, and the concept is now forgotten. Much of the rationale to not have a team assist in the launch was the notion of brand protection. The decision was to work on the business without the assistance of another to avoid allowing brand protection issues. Decisions such as these exist due to improper guidance and a company-facing perspective.

Leadership in Team-Building

The case study was an example of complete team avoidance and the negative ramifications of not having a team to assist in the progress. With a consciousness to utilize a full team for market entry, there are plenty of complexities for entrepreneurs and start-ups. Divergent thinking, learning orientation, and individual creative capacity produce different layers of belief and decision-making (Thayer et al. 2018). The value propositions held by the members may take time to reprogram to accomplish the goal of the company. Issues such as a task conflict, managing tension, challenges in development timing along with organizational practices contribute to the need for leadership in team building (Thayer et al. 2018). The entrepreneur is responsible for having a comprehensive plan to execute the product launch. This plan also includes the efforts of the selected team accounting for the skill and abilities of the members.

Different leadership styles will yield different results in the entrepreneur and start-up space. Democratic leadership decentralizes decision-making by sharing the responsibility among all pertinent members (Nagendra and Farooqui 2016). Start-ups forming a partnership and continuing the growth of the company with additional strategic partners may operate in this manner. The entrepreneur is the appointed leader by default but allows the other members to provide feedback and recommendations at an even level due to the expertise or another critical qualification. It is common for investors, legal teams, and creative managers to receive leadership privilege due to respect or reverence. Transformational leadership has four constructs created by Bass and Avolio (Jiang and Chen 2018).

1. Inspired motivation
2. Idealized influence
3. Individual consideration
4. Intellectual stimulation

The four constructs of transformational leadership provide an entrepreneur or a start-up founder with the ability to program around each particular member looking to maximize the skill of each member. The transformational leader will empower members to make decisions and work freely based on skill, passion, and expertise. The organizational culture will be conducive to progress as each member would share the collective goal and exercise open communication, collaboration, and cohesion. Transformational leadership works well in small business setting due to the size of the operation and the interaction of the appointed leader. The appointed leader can connect with each member pushing for a more significant opportunity for market entry. Strategy and execution are not separate disciplines but connects by goals of the entrepreneur. The team's ability and the available resources will play a large role in the decision-making for the leader (Reeves and di Carlo 2017). This specific leadership style works best as they do not dictate to the members in the traditional sense stifling the growth and adaptability of the team. The workflow and process is a dynamic interaction at the entrepreneurship level.

Case Study: Two Mobile Retail Platforms

Company A: A Retail Assistant Platform

A retail mobile assistant platform company was created (company name withheld) to assist consumers and retail stores with customer service and technical support issues. The purpose, business model, business strategy, and value proposition was outlined appropriately for a good product in the industry. The founder needed additional revenue to build more functionality into the platform along with creating a network for national integration into the retailers. The company was a two-person business without critical members assisting in fundraising, business development, marketing, and high-level platform coding. They were unable to realize a successful launch due to their small team.

Company B: AutoWallet©

AutoWallet© is a consolidated platform created to reduce the buying time in a dealership by 85 percent. This free tool will benefit the consumer by taking complex aspects of the vehicle purchase protocol and condensing into a simple, fun, and practical process. The viability report and feasibility study clearly outlined the consumer need with a robust value proposition. The team to bring this platform to market in late 2018 was assembled quickly by linking like-minded experts sharing the same passion. The founder is a seasoned serial entrepreneur with a history of successful product launches. Equity was given to two other members with the ability to code, build, program, integrate, and commercialize the platform. Multiple strategic partnerships allowed for rapid compliance and

Figure 6.1 AutoWallet© Welcome page

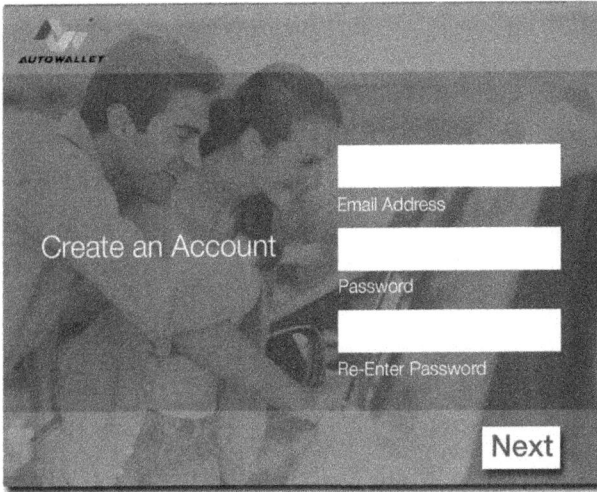

Figure 6.2 AutoWallet© Sign in page

regulatory adherence. Investment dollars were generated by the companies tech fund set up by the advisory board. The launch is spear-headed by a Fortune 500 company assisting in marketing and brand awareness. The usage of the team allowed AutoWallet© to have a rapid but effective opportunity for market entry.

Chapter 6 Review: Team Building for Execution

1. Shared beliefs and goals are the initial steps for team-building
2. Team-building consists of communication, collaboration, and cohesion creating the culture
3. The entrepreneur benefits from a strong team to avoid inadequate execution
4. Team members can be any of the following:
   (a) Entrepreneur/Founder
   (b) Operations
   (c) Chief Financial Officer
   (d) Chief Technical Officer
   (e) Business Development
   (f) Commercial Development
   (g) Marketing and Advertising

(h) Legal

(i) Investors

(j) Performers/Assistants

5. Transformational and democratic leadership styles benefit entrepreneurship teams

CHAPTER 7

Minimum Viable Product (MVP)

The planning and preparation completed by the entrepreneur or small business owner lead to development and release of the minimum viable product. The innovation creates a minimum viable product based on the information collected in the viability report and feasibility study along with the real purpose and value proposition. The minimum viable product (MVP) is the least expensive created product or service released to the market while making a profit. Development of the MVP begins the real-world learning process by integrating the early adopters' feedback as quickly as possible (Lenarduzzi and Taibi 2016). The time frame from concept to delivery of the MVP needs to be quick but not rushed. The information gathered through the studies and reporting assists in decision-making. A competitive advantage for entrepreneurs and small businesses as compared to large organizations is the ability to move fast and adapt to changing circumstances (Duc and Abrahamsson 2016). Small businesses and entrepreneurs struggle with resources, brand recognition, and reach. As of result of these limitations, the MVP bodes well for innovation and proper market entry. As a cost and time-saving vehicle, the MVP offers the ability to learn about the consumer climate while offering value.

Beta Testing

The business model, business strategy, viability report, and feasibility study lead to the MVP and the timing for the concept, product, or service launch. Following changing consumer requests, competitor activity, technology or regulatory shifts, fluid, and an easily adaptable plan is used for a proper product entry (Barden 2018). Founders and start-ups benefit by thinking in highly flexible ways. The main point is to develop an MVP that can be tested by consumers and pivoted if necessary around consumer value propositions revealed through an interactive process to gain successful feedback (Rasmussen and Tanev 2016). Beta-testing prepares the path for the entrepreneur as the development of the MVP ensues. The subsequent implementation of commercialization strategies using similar conditions, costs, and risk factors of a launch is a proper measurement of product, concept, or service reaction by the target audience (Marx and Hsu 2015). The benefit of beta-testing is the acceleration of a concept and the diffusion of issues before a significant loss occurs. Reliability-related and market-related benefits are developed through models to determine the optimal path for market entry leading to an appropriate expectation of economies of scope (Jiang, Scheibe, Nilakanta, and Qu 2017). The continued learning the knowledge provided by the exercise of beta-testing is invaluable in preventing unnecessary cost and product misplacement. Beta-testing reveals product behavior in the marketplace, performance traits, accuracy aspects, marketing opportunity, additional features, fix-times, and creates innovation awareness (Kumar and Abraham 2017). Beta-testing reshapes the expectations for the final product and provides the idea for evolving opportunities, while reducing stress in product launches, solving consumer problems, and increasing consumer buy in (Shueh 2016).

Case Study: JetFuel Tech® Wearables

As an Ohio-based company, JetFuel Tech® specializes in innovative and unique technology products enhancing safety and performance for athletes. The flagship products is a wearable technology measuring heart-rate, posture, respiration, and respiration rate in conjunction with standard mobile device or smartphone. This product was created in Japan and commercialized in the United States. The beta-testing phase included early adopters in the professional sports realm, the United States Air Force, and medical staff in the Midwest. The testing revealed the appropriate use in the market and additional products for commercialization. The wearable transitioned from a shirt to a sports bra and compression shorts along with additional sensors in wristbands and socks to measure motion and

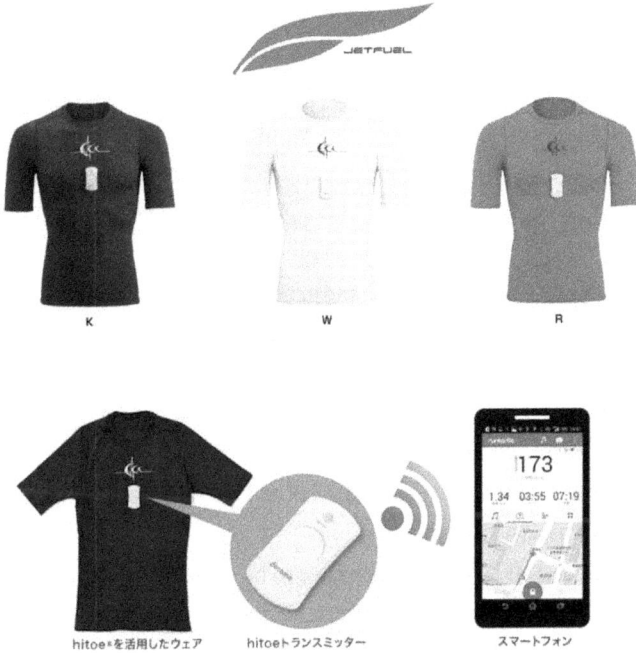

Figure 7.1 JetFuel Tech® Wearable: Hitoe©

range. The exercise of beta-testing created partnerships with the NFL, NBA, and many prominent companies due to the value proposition and efficiency of use. The wearable technology boasted orders at the onset of the market entry due to the successful beta-testing stage.

Development of the MVP

The development of the MVP has many layers due to the features deemed most important by the entrepreneur, information from the viability report and feasibility study, and the feedback from the beta-test. Ultimately the advancement of the MVP is achieved by avoiding waste and time-consuming features. The versions to test and validate ideas emerge to eliminate the wasteful creation of complicated products as a measure to streamline the entry process (Duc and Abrahamsson 2016). The previously gathered information from the report and study lead to quicker decision-making in the development and launch of the MVP. Creating a full-featured product or service uses more resources to accomplish costing valuable market time while increasing risk on return. During the MVP stage, the goal is to identify early adopters to use the product or service is a manner conducive to understanding, adjustment, and scale (Loveys 2018). In previous times, businesses would spend more time looking to create a completed project and unveiling to the public at the conclusion of the creation. This methodology was expensive and slow-moving although the consumers received a comprehensive and finished product. Current trends determine small and more manageable aspects highlighting consumer feedback through low fidelity prototypes, mock-ups, and storyboards of a product is more acceptable and necessary than larger more comprehensive projects (Barden 2018). The concentration of the entrepreneur and small business owner is to research thoroughly in order to develop quickly. The agile and flexible method will capture the consumer interest and value proposition.

Developing an MVP does not have to be a complicated process. There are four elements of primary concern for the entrepreneur.

1. Consumers
2. Value proposition
3. Channels
4. Relationships

These four elements ensure the entrepreneur maintains focus on the development of a consumer-facing innovation. Concentrating on the benefit to the consumer leads to an MVP developed in a recognizable and user-friendly way readily accepted by the consumer market. The value proposition ensures the consumers will use the innovation also leading to monetization for the company. The channel development concentrates on how to distribute the innovation to the consumer market during entry. Establishing good relationships with strategic partners, the consumer market, and complementary companies increase the percentages of a successful MVP launch. Each one of these elements is important and vital to developing an MVP worthy of an appropriate entry.

There are a classic quality and a product quality to the development of an MVP. The classic quality is the traditional rational analysis derived from the entrepreneur or small business owner. This concept, product,

Table 7.1 Aspects of a good MVP

Tangible elements	Intangible elements
Visual experience	Likable
Distinguishing characteristics	Easy to understand
Easy to use	Novel and fresh
Familiar elements	Reliable and credible
Integration and access	Personal connectivity

or service is broken down into subcomponents and demonstrate clear mechanics in operation or delivery. The classic quality is essential for understanding how the product works and its usage in the consumer market. The product quality is the understanding of the overall feel and holistic approach to the concept, product or service. The emotions, passion, and belief surrounding the innovation are articulated and demonstrated in this quality of the MVP. Consumers connect to emotional aspects of products which bring forth levels of affinity establishing brand loyalty. The product quality development of the MVP creates long-term loyal consumers when executed appropriately.

The aspects of a good MVP are illustrated in Table 7.1.

Case Study: Two Mobile Platform Companies

Company A: A Platform Company

A technology platform company was created (company name withheld) to provide tech solutions for the general public and small businesses. The innovation would force interaction between the two entities in a method not previously known. Conceptually the platform is novel, creative, and fits an immediate need for a particular segment of the market. The intended target audience is not familiar with the delivery method, terminology, or return on interaction according to the viability report and feasibility study. The created MVP lacks identification in the four primary elements as the distribution channels, and the relationships prove to be challenging to execute and articulate. The MVP suffers from providing legitimate value to the consumer which is also causing entry issues for the company.

Company B: RATSM Concepts® ProElite Training©

ProElite Training is a consolidated mobile application used to train athletes through the metronome of music to increase rhythm, tempo, and pace. RATSM Concepts is an acronym for Rhythm Athletic Training Systems Method Concept which is the name of the intellectual property. ProElite Training boasts the ability to offer training for free to athletes, fans, and sports enthusiasts globally in conjunction with a smartphone or mobile device. Premium content is $9.99 or $19.99 on a subscription model. The premium content features players from the NFL, NBA, MLS, along with professional boxers and mixed martial art fighters. Premium content also allows for customized workouts, augmented reality, virtual reality, social connectivity, and unlimited licensed streamed music. The MVP features only three of the six available sports, only 15 total athletes as opposed to the 100 available athletes, no augmented or virtual reality and a limited song selection. The viability report and feasibility study along with the beta suggested the MVP was adequate for scale and consumer appreciation. The revealings produced a rapid development while saving millions of dollars in the process.

Figure 7.2 RATSM concept® ProElite training© Intro

Figure 7.3 ProElite training© Marketing page

Table 7.2 Benefit of an MVP

Benefits of an MVP	
✓ Quick initiation and engagement	✓ Leads to scope and scale
✓ Provides viability data	✓ Provides just-in-time inventory
✓ Creates brand awareness	✓ Ability to develop over time
✓ Establishes a consumer base	✓ Adjust with substitutes and complements
✓ Allows for real time learning	✓ Evolution of consumer experience

Chapter 7 Review: Minimum Viable Product

1. The MVP is the least expensive created product or service released to the market while making a profit
2. Beta-testing reveals product behavior and reshapes expectations for entry
3. The MVP reduces waste and increases the time to market for feedback
4. There are four primary elements of an MVP: Consumer, value, channels, and relationship

CHAPTER 8

Performance for Success

Starting a company or launching a product is not an easy task for any individual, even a tenured serial entrepreneur. The pre-planning, research, testing, trial, and error stages can be difficult for entrepreneurs to survive. The time commitment, associated costs, and ever-changing market conditions leave doubt in the minds of many small business owners. There is no specific pathway guaranteeing success with innovation development. The steps outlined in the book are to minimize considerable obstacles and unnecessary waste. Start-up founders embark on a new concept, product, or service to achieve success with their passion or skill. Conscious but adventurous action by the entrepreneur maximizes the opportunity for success regarding the innovation.

Defining Success

The concept of success carries a different meaning due to the dynamic and broad perception of success. Entrepreneurs, start-up founders, and small business owners define success differently in many cases. One reason for the ambiguous definition of success is the concept has many characteristics explaining various aspects. Based on psychological research concerning entrepreneur or founder success there are eight characteristics according to Agnes and Benedicta Prihatin Dwi (2017).

1. Product integration
2. Market scope
3. Age of business
4. Size of team
5. Financial resources
6. Marketing range

7. Added experience
8. Intellectual property

In addition to these eight psychological factors self-efficacy, innovation, proactivity, confidence, resiliency, and independence are personality factors (Agnes and Benedicta PrihatinDwi 2017). Product integration is a measure of success as one goal for any founder or entrepreneur is to have their product or concept incorporated into the mainstream in a meaningful way. An example of integration is AutoWallet© integrating into the systems of dealerships nationwide for mandated use or RoleTea© receiving shelf space from the Whole Foods Mid-Atlantic region. In either instance, the integration demonstrates a good market entry success. The increased market scope is also another measure of success due to the ramifications of future progress. Increasing markets are a good sign of increased opportunity. The Alum Clock© has an increased market scope with the licensing agreements with Learfield® which is responsible for over 650 major college institutions nationwide. The partnership increases the market for the SPI Products® and the Alum Clock©.

The age of the business represents longevity and the propensity for sustainability. Some innovations are created to "flip" after demonstrating proof of concept, but many entrepreneurs are looking to establish their business in a significant manner. The four-year age of NeXgen Vapors® demonstrates success in the longevity category offering hope and confidence for continued progress. The size of the team is a measurement of success as the growth of the team offers more talent and ability to reach more consumers. Financial resources are a marker of success for any business at any stage. When revenues are increasing over periods of time, that is, a direct correlation to a successful strategy or trend, the marketing range measures the depth and breadth of the consumer base. As the market share enlarges, the opportunities to capture the market share are directly proportionate, leading to increased success. Added experience through real-world scenarios provides more knowledge, skill, and confidence for future ventures. Experience is invaluable when recognized and used appropriately. Developing intellectual property such as a patent or a trademark is an exciting accomplishment for many. The development is a successful contribution to the world and knowledge as a whole.

Success is also the consideration of significant returns to the stakeholder collaborators. Through the Whole-Brain Thinking Method, stakeholders are looking for a return on investment, implementation, innovation, or interaction (Whole Brain 2017). Ensuring a return on one of the four concepts is a sure way to determine a successful product entry. Providing value to the consumers in a recognizable and precise method is another way to analyze success for the entrepreneur. Each aspect explained is a measurement of success through the entrepreneur or founder performance. Performance is the capability to attain objectives in an expected or superior manner through various perspectives (Caseiro and Coelho 2018). The various perspectives exist because time frames, team members influence, and stakeholders expectations vary tremendously. The needs or unmet consumer needs, external opportunities, and complementary innovation will continue to drive adjustment, reevaluation, and new goals (Legenvre and Gualandris 2018). The multifaceted approach allows the entrepreneur to find small wins and substantial successes throughout the MVP process.

Continued Exploration of Success

Success for an entrepreneur or a founder does not end with the development of an MVP. The life cycle of a venture consists of the start-up, transition, scale, and exit (Picken 2018). The MVP gets the entrepreneur a start on growing the business into a significant entity. The transition goes from uncertainty to confidence due to the feedback on the innovation created. Scaling the business is another term for growing the business. This growth comes in the form of adding organizational members, investing more financial resources, or adding products and services. The exit is strategic and selected. Larger companies purchase smaller companies in good financial standing or riding promising upward trends. The entrepreneur will succeed in more areas if the goal is to travel through the four-stage life cycle. Creating a sound MVP will set the occasion for the desired success. Every entrepreneur looking to succeed will emphasize the process of exploration, validation, and refinement of the business concept and the MVP (Picken 2018). This process will keep the founder or entrepreneur on pace for understanding the progress of the MVP and how to make corrections for enhanced performance.

The MVP provides one standard for entrepreneur success in innovation, but there are multiple methods of measuring goal performance and achievement. Three types of organizational performance measurement are financial performance, conceptualization, and organizational effectiveness (Caseiro and Coelho 2018). These methods are not only more ambiguous but also standard ways of evaluating the early success for a start-up or entrepreneur. Financial performance is a direct outcome-based measure which may not be an accurate determination of success; however, it is the most critical. Receiving finances through investments or revenue will always exist as a critical factor for a business. Finances are the lifeline of any company and the overall sustaining factor. Conceptualization deals with aspects such as product-market outcomes, market share, and additional product placement (Caseiro and Coelho 2018). The mentality regarding this measurement is providing a more holistic look at the contributions the business is making to the market for renewed opportunity capitalization. Organizational effectiveness relates to aspects such as reputation, survival, achievement, and overall performance (Caseiro and Coelho 2018). Combining the three types of organizational

Table 8.1 Reminders for developing a successful MVP

Reminders for developing a successful MVP
Set a Direction: Maintain Focus
Properly Position Product
Maintain Consumer Responsiveness
Build an Effective Team
Develop a Process
Build Financial Capability
Develop the Appropriate Culture
Manage Risks and Vulnerabilities

measurements allows the entrepreneur to compare and contrast efforts in regards to the MVP and sustainability.

It is essential the entrepreneur be accountable for the successes during the journey of getting to the market with their MVP as there are many challenges in the start-up space. There are challenges to define and validate the business concept, market the innovation, provide a timely offering, develop a go-to-market strategy, and incorporate consumer feedback (Picken 2018). To avoid discouragement and distraction, the entrepreneur benefits from remaining organized and focused on where the data recommends. Managing the risks in acceptable ways, while minimizing the damage of unexpected obstacles is critical.

Chapter 8 Review: Performance for Success

1. Success carries many meanings due to the dynamic understanding
2. There are eight stable characteristics for success
   (a) Product integration
   (b) Market scope
   (c) Age of business
   (d) Size of team
   (e) Financial resources
   (f) Marketing range
   (g) Added experience
   (h) Intellectual property
3. Success provides a return on investment, implementation, innovation, or interaction
4. Start-up, transition, scale, and exit
5. Find small wins to maintain momentum for a successful MVP entry

Conclusion

The idea of creating a new concept, product, or service is exciting and stressful simultaneously. Many cultural and market phenomenon inspire innovation. The goal of the founder, entrepreneur, or small business owner is to reduce the associated risk with innovation launches by developing a sound MVP for market entry. The purpose of the innovation will outline the "why" the innovation should exist and is essential. Recognizing the opportunity in the marketplace is a careful and conscious analysis by the entrepreneur. This stage sets the occasion for operational and organizational strategy. Creating the concept shapes the definition of the dream to appropriately research aspects surrounding the passion. The viability report and feasibility study formalizes the process and adds legitimate information for sound decision-making during development. The entrepreneur will revisit the concept to ensure the value proposition is consumer-facing and beneficial for the stakeholder collaborators. This step increases the percentage of longevity and better market entry. Building a competent team to bring the concept, product, or service to fruition is vital and critical to long-term success. All of the preparation and analysis lead to the development of the MVP. The MVP provides quick and agile movement in the marketplace with the least amount of associated cost and risk. The MVP will provide feedback from the consumer market leading to adjustment and correction. Once the MVP is complete, the time is to perform and prepare for sustainability. The challenges of entrepreneurship do not have to be a deterrent when the appropriate tools, passion, and knowledge are applied.

References

Dessyana, A., and B.P.D. Riyanti. 2017. "The Influence of Innovation and Entrepreneurial Self-Efficacy to Digital Startup Success." *International Research Journal of Business Studies* 10, no. 1, 57–68. doi:10.21632/irjbs.10.1.57-68

Ahmad, M.M. 2017. "(Meta) Cognition in Comprehension: Understanding Multimodal Processing." *FWU Journal of Social Sciences* 11, no. 1, pp. 148–62.

Ashley, S., H. Schaap, and E. de Bruijn. 2016. "Defining Conceptual Understanding for Teaching in International Business." *Journal of Teaching in International Business* 27, no. 2, pp. 106–23.

Atsan, N. 2016. "Failure Experiences of Entrepreneurs: Causes and Learning Outcomes." *Procedia-Social and Behavioral Sciences*, 235(12th International Strategic Management Conference, ISMC 2016, October 28–30, 2016, Antalya, Turkey), 435–42. doi:10.1016/j.sbspro.2016.11.054

Badgett, K. February 1, 2018. "School-Business Partnerships: Understanding Business Perspectives." *National Forum of Applied Educational Research Journal* 31, pp. 83–105.

Banu, G.S., A. Dumitrescu, A.A. Purcărea, and S.W. Isărescu. 2016. "Defining Open Innovation Concept Using Business Process Modeling." *Procedia. Technology*, 22(9th International Conference Interdisciplinarity in Engineering, INTER-ENG 2015, October 8–9, 2015, Tirgu Mures, Romania), 1020–27. doi:10.1016/j.protcy.2016.01.135

Barden, E. 2018. "What's the Agile Got to Do With It? Seven Key Trends Leaders Need to Know." *NZ Business + Management* 32, no. 4, (Sp)22–(Sp)25.

Barraket, J., C. Furneaux, S. Barth, and C. Mason. 2016. "Understanding Legitimacy Formation in Multi-Goal Firms: An Examination of Business Planning Practices Among Social Enterprises." *Journal of Small Business Management*, 5477–89. doi:10.1111/jsbm.12290

Biloshapka, V., and O. Osiyevskyy. 2018. "Three Value-Focused Strategic Questions for Continuously Updating Your Business Model." *Strategy & Leadership* 46, no. 3, 45–51. doi:10.1108/SL-02-2018-0016

Caseiro, N., and A. Coelho. 2018. "Empirical Paper: The Influence of Business Intelligence Capacity, Network Learning and Innovativeness on Startups Performance." *Journal of Innovation & Knowledge*. doi:10.1016/j.jik.2018.03.009

Choi, N., S. Shin, S.U. Song, and J. Sung. 2018. "Minoxidil Promotes Hair Growth Through Stimulation of Growth Factor Release From

Adipose-Derived Stem Cells." *International Journal of Molecular Sciences* 19, no. 3, 1-N.PAG. doi:10.3390/ijms19030691

Chun-Lan, C. 2015. "Entrepreneurial Orientation, Communication Strategies, and New Product Success: A Theoretical Model." *Academy of Strategic Management Journal* 14, no. 1, pp. 1–19.

Derbyshire, J., and E. Giovannetti. 2017. "Understanding the Failure to Understand New Product Development Failures: Mitigating the Uncertainty Associated with Innovating New Products by Combining Scenario Planning and Forecasting." *Technological Forecasting & Social Change* 125, 334–44. doi:10.1016/j.techfore.2017.02.007

Dhebar, A. 2016. "Bringing New High-technology Products to Market: Six Perils Awaiting Marketers." *Business Horizons* 59 (Cybersecurity in 2016: People, Technology, and Processes), 713–22. doi:10.1016/j.bushor.2016.08.006

Duc A., and P. Abrahamsson. 2016. "Minimum Viable Product or Multiple Facet Product? The Role of MVP in Software Startups." *Agile Processes, In Software Engineering & Extreme Programming* (9783319335148).

Forsström-Tuominen, H., I. Jussila, and S. Goel. 2017. "The Start of Team Start-ups: Collective Dynamics of Initiation and Formation of Entrepreneurial Teams." *Journal Of Enterprising Culture* 25, no. 1, 31–66. doi:10.1142/S0218495817500029

Gans, J., E.L. Scott, and S. Stern. 2018. "Strategy for Start-ups." *Harvard Business Review* 96, no. 3, pp. 44–51.

Gill, M., S. Sridhar, and R. Grewal. 2017. "Return on Engagement Initiatives: A Study of a Business-to-Business Mobile App." *Journal of Marketing* 81, no. 4, 45–66. doi:10.1509/jm.16.0149

Goswami, M., and M.K. Tiwari. 2015. "Product Feature and Functionality Driven Integrated Framework for Product Commercialization in Presence of Qualitative Consumer Reviews." *International Journal of Production Research* 53, no. 16, 4769–88. doi:10.1080/00207543.2014.987358

Greene, F.J., and C. Hopp. 2018. "When Should Entrepreneurs Write their Business Plans?" *Harvard Business Review Digital Articles*, pp. 2–4.

Grover, V., R.L. Chiang, L. Ting-Peng, and Z. Dongsong. 2018. "Creating Strategic Business Value from Big Data Analytics: A Research Framework." *Journal of Management Information Systems* 35, no. 2, 388–423. doi:10.1080/07421222.2018.1451951

Harvey, A. 2016. "This Is How the Smartest Entrepreneurs Lead Teams." *Fortune. Com*, no. 1.

Healey, M.P., and G.P. Hodgkinson. 2017. "Making Strategy Hot." *California Management Review* 59, no. 3, 109–34. doi:10.1177/0008125617712258

Houlder, D., and N. Nandkishore. 2016. "4 Hard Questions to Ask About Your Company's Purpose." *Harvard Business Review Digital Articles*, pp. 2–4.

Husen, S. 2017. "The Mediating Role of Product Positioning Quality and Product Attractiveness Advantage." *International Journal of Business & Management Science* 7, no. 1, pp. 1–10.

Jiang, Y., and C.C. Chen. 2018. "Integrating Knowledge Activities for Team Innovation: Effects of Transformational Leadership." *Journal of Management* 44, no. 5, pp. 1819–47.

Jiang, Z., K.P. Scheibe, S. Nilakanta, and X. Qu. 2017. "The Economics of Public Beta Testing." *Decision Sciences* 48, no. 1, 150–75. doi:10.1111/deci.12221

Jimenez-Jimenez, D., M. Martinez-Costa, and H. Ahmed-Dine Rabeh. 2018. "Fostering New Product Success Through Learning Competences." *Technology Analysis & Strategic Management* 30, no. 1, pp. 58–70.

Kumar, A., and A. Abraham. 2017. "Opinion Mining to Assist User Acceptance Testing for Open-Beta Versions." *Journal of Information Assurance & Security* 12, no. 4, pp. 146–53.

Lecours, M. 2017. "Developing a Framework to Craft a Value Proposition." *Journal of Financial Planning* 30, no. 3, pp. 23–25.

Lee, M., and S. Lee. 2017. "Identifying New Business Opportunities from Competitor Intelligence: An Integrated Use of Patent and Trademark Databases." *Technological Forecasting & Social Change* 119, 170–83. doi:10.1016/j.techfore.2017.03.026

Legenvre, H., and J. Gualandris. 2018. "Innovation Sourcing Excellence: Three Purchasing Capabilities for Success." *Business Horizons* 61, 95–106. doi:10.1016/j.bushor.2017.09.009

Lejeck, D.W. 2017. "Team Building: Without the Three Cs, You don't Really have a Team." *Smart Business Pittsburgh* 24, no. 5, p. 10.

Lenarduzzi, V., and D. Taibi. 2016. "MVP Explained: A Systematic Mapping Study on the Definitions of Minimal Viable Product." *42th Euromicro Conference on Software Engineering and Advanced Applications (SEAA).* doi:10.1109/SEAA.2016.56

Loveys, M. 2018. "Garage to Global." *NZ Business + Management* 32, no. 3, pp. 26–27.

Mata-Lima, H., A. Alvino-Borba, K. Akamatsu, B. Incau, J. Jard, A.B. da Silva, and F. Morgado-Dias. 2016. "Measuring an Organization's Performance: The Road to Defining Sustainability Indicators." *Environmental Quality Management* 26, no. 2, 89–104. doi:10.1002/tqem.21487

Marx, M., and D.H. Hsu. 2015. "Strategic Switchbacks: Dynamic Commercialization Strategies for Technology Entrepreneurs." *Research Policy* 44, 1815–26. doi:10.1016/j.respol.2015.06.016

Morgan, B., J. Hejdenberg, S. Hinrichs-Krapels, and D. Armstrong. 2018. "Do Feasibility Studies Contribute to, or Avoid, Waste in Research?" *Plos One* 13, no. 3, 1–8. doi:10.1371/journal.pone.0195951

Muff, K. 2017. "How the Circle Model Can Purpose-orient Entrepreneurial Universities and Business Schools to Truly Serve Society." *Journal of Management Development* 36, no. 2, 146–62. doi:10.1108/JMD-06-2016-0120

Murray, B. 2016. "How Distributors Drive Innovation." *Music Trades* 163, no. 12, pp. 72–77.

Nagendra, A., and S. Farooqui. 2016. "Role of Leadership Style on Organizational Performance." *CLEAR International Journal of Research In Commerce & Management* 7, no. 4, pp. 65–67.

Napoli, J., S. Dickinson-Delaporte, and M.B. Beverland. 2016. "The Brand Authenticity Continuum: Strategic Approaches for Building Value." *Journal of Marketing Management* 32, 13–14, 1201–29. doi:10.1080/0267257X.2016.1145722

Ogbari, M.E., A.S. Ibidunni, O.O. Ogunnaike, M.A. Olokundun, and A.B. Amaihian. 2018. "A Comparative Analysis of Small Business Strategic Orientation: Implications for Performance." *Academy of Strategic Management Journal* 17, no. 1, pp. 1–15.

Picken, J.C. 2018. "From Startup to Scalable Enterprise: Laying the Foundation." *Business Horizons* 60, no. 5, pp. 587–95.

Ploum, L., V. Blok, T. Lans, and O. Omta. 2018. "Exploring the Relation Between Individual Moral Antecedents and Entrepreneurial Opportunity Recognition for Sustainable Development." *Journal of Cleaner Production* 172, 1582–91. doi:10.1016/j.jclepro.2017.10.296

Prause, G. 2015. "Sustainable Business Models and Structures for Industry 4.0." *Journal of Security & Sustainability Issues* 5, no. 2, 159–69. doi:10.9770/jssi.2015.5.2(3)

Rasmussen, E., and S. Tanev. 2016. "3: Lean Start-up. Making the Start-up More Successful." *Start-up Creation*, 39–56. doi:10.1016/B978-0-08-100546-0.00003-0

Reeves, M., and R.C. Di Carlo. 2017. "Your Strategy has to be Flexible—But So Does Your Execution." *Harvard Business Review Digital Articles*, pp. 2–5.

Riihimäki, T., V. Kaartemo, and P. Zettinig. 2016. "Co-evolution of Dynamic Capabilities and Value Propositions from a Process Perspective." *Advances In Business-Related Scientific Research Journal* 7, no. 1, pp. 63–76.

Rintamäki, T., and K. Kirves. 2017. "From Perceptions to Propositions: Profiling Customer Value Across Retail Contexts." *Journal of Retailing & Consumer Services* 37,159–67. doi:10.1016/j.jretconser.2016.07.016

Robbins, P., and C. O'Gorman. 2016. "Innovation Processes: Do They Help or Hinder New Product Development Outcomes in Irish SMEs?" *Irish Journal of Management* 35, no. 1, 104–07. doi:10.1515/ijm-2016-0006

Ruygrok, C.M. 2016. "Building a Strong Team Culture for Sustained Performance." *AAACN Viewpoint* 38, no. 1, pp. 14–15.

Santos, S.C., A. Caetano, S.F. Costa, S.C. Santos, and D. Wach. 2018. "Recognizing Opportunities Across Campus: The Effects of Cognitive Training and Entrepreneurial Passion on the Business Opportunity Prototype." *Journal of Small Business Management* 56, no. 1, pp. 51–75.

Schramm, C. 2018. "It's not about the Framework." *Harvard Business Review* 96, no. 3, pp. 52–54.

Shueh, J. 2016. "Reshaping Expectations." *Government Technology* 29, no. 6, pp. 38–39.

Souto, J.E. 2015. "Business Model Innovation and Business Concept Innovation as the Context of Incremental Innovation and Radical Innovation." *Tourism Management* 51, pp. 142–55.

Štefan, S., and Z. Branislav. 2016. "Relationship Between Business Strategy and Business Model Studied in a Sample of Service Companies." *Journal of Competitiveness* 8, no. 4, 72–84. doi:10.7441/joc.2016.04.05

Thayer, A.L., A. Petruzzelli, and C.E. McClurg. 2018. "Addressing the Paradox of the Team Innovation Process: A Review and Practical Considerations." *American Psychologist* 73, no. 4, 363–75. doi:10.1037/amp0000310

Vogan, M. 2017. "Moody's Analytics. Electrical Vehicle Residual Value Outlook." Retrieved from moodysanalytics.com/-/media/presentation/2017/electric-vehicle-residual-value-outlook.pdf

Wei, F. 2017. "An Approach to Evaluating the Knowledge Innovation Ability of New Ventures Based on Knowledge Management with Fuzzy Number Intuitionistic Fuzzy Information." *Journal Of Intelligent & Fuzzy Systems* 32, no. 6, 4357–65. doi:10.3233/JIFS-16731

Whole-Brain Thinking. 2017. *BizEd* 16, no. 5, p. 65.

Wouters, M., J.C. Anderson, and M. Kirchberger. 2018. "New-Technology Startups Seeking Pilot Customers: Crafting a Pair of Value Propositions." *California Management Review* 60, no. 4, 101–24. doi:10.1177/0008125618778855

Yang, D., L. Jin, and S. Sheng. 2017. "The Effect of Knowledge Breadth and Depth on New Product Performance." *International Journal of Market Research* 59, no. 4, 517–36. doi:10.2501/IJMR-2017-007

About the Author

J.C. Baker is the founder and CEO of J.C. Baker & Associates (jcbaker.org) a business consulting firm in Cincinnati, Ohio. As a number one Amazon best-selling author and a four-time published author, J.C. Baker has written about logic, spiritual matters, and business leadership. With 20 years of high-level sales, entrepreneurship, and consulting experience, he has been successful in a diverse range of industries such as tech, retail, education, and automotive. J.C. Baker is an expert in organizational strategy and process innovation. He is also a content creator for CBT News and the Atlanta Small Business Network while performing duties as an Entrepreneur in Residence at the University of Cincinnati's 1819 Innovation Hub. He also serves as an advisor on the Ohio State University and Central State University Extension Board. He received his BA in History from the University of Cincinnati, with his MBA and Doctorate in Business and Organizational Leadership coming from Northcentral University in California.

Index

OTHER TITLES IN THE ENTREPRENEURSHIP AND SMALL BUSINESS MANAGEMENT COLLECTION

Scott Shane, Case Western University, Editor

- *African American Entrepreneurs: Successes and Struggles of Entrepreneurs of Color in America* by Michelle Ingram Spain and J. Mark Munoz
- *How to Get Inside Someone's Mind and Stay There: The Small Business Owner's Guide to Content Marketing and Effective Message Creation* by Jacky Fitt
- *Profit: Plan for It, Get It—The Entrepreneurs Handbook* by H.R Hutter
- *Understanding the Family Business: Exploring the Differences Between Family and Nonfamily Businesses, Second Edition* by Keanon J. Alderson
- *Navigating Entrepreneurship: 11 Proven Keys to Success* by Larry Jacobson
- *Global Women in the Start-up World: Conversations in Silicon Valley* by Marta Zucker

Announcing the Business Expert Press Digital Library

Concise e-books business students need for classroom and research

This book can also be purchased in an e-book collection by your library as

- a one-time purchase,
- that is owned forever,
- allows for simultaneous readers,
- has no restrictions on printing, and
- can be downloaded as PDFs from within the library community.

Our digital library collections are a great solution to beat the rising cost of textbooks. E-books can be loaded into their course management systems or onto students' e-book readers.
The **Business Expert Press** digital libraries are very affordable, with no obligation to buy in future years. For more information, please visit **www.businessexpertpress.com/librarians**. To set up a trial in the United States, please email **sales@businessexpertpress.com**.